How Schools Meet
Students' Needs

Critical Issues in American Education

Lisa M. Nunn, Series Editor

Taking advantage of sociology's position as a leader in the social scientific study of education, this series is home to new empirical and applied bodies of work that combine social analysis, cultural critique, and historical perspectives across disciplinary lines and the usual methodological boundaries. Books in the series aim for topical and theoretical breadth. Anchored in sociological analysis, Critical Issues in American Education features carefully crafted empirical work that takes up the most pressing educational issues of our time, including federal education policy, gender and racial disparities in student achievement, access to higher education, labor market outcomes, teacher quality, and decision making within institutions.

Judson G. Everitt, *Lesson Plans: The Institutional Demands of Becoming a Teacher*

Megan M. Holland, *Divergent Paths to College: Race, Class, and Inequality in High Schools*

Katie Kerstetter, *How Schools Meet Students' Needs: Inequality, School Reform, and Caring Labor*

Laura Nichols, *The Journey Before Us: First-Generation Pathways from Middle School to College*

Lisa M. Nunn, *College Belonging: How First-Year and First-Generation Students Navigate Campus Life*

Daisy Verduzco Reyes, *Learning to Be Latino: How Colleges Shape Identity Politics*

How Schools Meet Students' Needs

Inequality, School Reform,
and Caring Labor

KATIE KERSTETTER

Rutgers University Press

New Brunswick, Camden, and Newark, New Jersey, and London

Library of Congress Cataloging-in-Publication Data
Names: Kerstetter, Katie, author.
Title: How schools meet students' needs : inequality, school reform, and caring labor /
    Katie Kerstetter.
Description: New Brunswick : Rutgers University Press, [2023] | Series: Critical
    issues in American education | Includes bibliographical references and index.
Identifiers: LCCN 2022010607 | ISBN 9781978823594 (hardback) | ISBN
    9781978823587 (paperback) | ISBN 9781978823600 (epub) | ISBN
    9781978823617 (mobi) | ISBN 9781978823624 (pdf)
Subjects: LCSH: School management and organization—United States. |
    Educational equalization—United States. | Educational change—United
    States. | Social learning—United States. | School children—Social
    conditions—United States.
Classification: LCC LB2805 .K45 2023 | DDC 379.2/60973—dc23/eng/20220521
LC record available at https://lccn.loc.gov/2022010607

A British Cataloging-in-Publication record for this book is available from the British Library.

References to internet websites (URLs) were accurate at the time of writing. Neither the
author nor Rutgers University Press is responsible for URLs that may have expired or changed
since the manuscript was prepared.

♾ The paper used in this publication meets the requirements of the American National
Standard for Information Sciences—Permanence of Paper for Printed Library Materials,
ANSI Z39.48-1992.

www.rutgersuniversitypress.org

Manufactured in the United States of America

Contents

How Schools Meet
Students' Needs

Introduction

• •

On an April morning in Ms. Lesley's kindergarten classroom, a group of children are seated on the carpet at the front of the classroom. Ms. Lesley, a petite woman with shoulder-length, light-brown hair who identifies as White and female, has been teaching at Oak Grove for the past decade. Ms. Lesley places her hands on Rashaad's legs and encourages him quietly to sit in "criss-cross apple sauce." Rashaad, a student whom I perceived to be Black and male,[1] is wearing the school uniform of a white polo shirt and long khaki shorts. He looks upset and sits quietly for a few moments before slowly moving his legs into a cross-legged position.

Ms. Lesley reads the morning message to the students and then, in a whisper, asks the students to go to centers or their reading groups. Amber, a student whom I perceived to be Black and female and whose dark hair is gathered into two braids, walks with Rashaad over to a c-shaped table to meet with Ms. Lesley. Their teacher passes out two copies of the same book. Amber begins to read her copy of the book aloud, while Rashaad sits silently.

Ms. Lesley puts a blue divider up between the two students, creating some privacy. "Can you tell me what's wrong?" Ms. Lesley asks Rashaad, placing her forearms on top of his arms. Rashaad responds quietly, so quietly that it is difficult to hear his response from a few feet away. "Can you speak a little louder?" Ms. Lesley encourages him and leans in to listen to what he is saying. This time, I can hear the Rashaad's voice but can't make out what he is saying. "Oh, well that is why we have to eat breakfast over our desks," Ms. Lesley says in response to what Rashaad is explaining. "Why don't we do reading group first and then if you're still hungry we can have a snack afterwards?"

Appearing to agree, Rashaad begins to read his book aloud, and Ms. Lesley helps him with the last page. "Does that say 'in the bed?' Try again," she encourages him. "I am in bed," Rashaad re-reads. "Excellent job!" Ms. Lesley responds.

Ms. Lesley asks Rashaad and Amber if they remember where the main character of their book was playing. After they answer, she asks them if they remember what they told her yesterday about where they liked to play. "In a tent," Amber says. "Yes," Ms. Lesley agrees, and gives Amber a strip of paper that has "I am in the tent" handwritten on it. Rashaad says that he likes to play in a different place than what is written on his sentence strip, and Ms. Lesley reminds him that he said that he liked to play in trees on Monday. Ms. Lesley asks Rashaad and Amber to read their personalized sentences aloud. Then, she takes a pair of scissors and cuts the sentence strip into pieces so that each word is a separate piece. Rashaad rubs his eyes as if he is tired. Ms. Lesley shuffles the words around, and Rashaad and Amber work to reconstruct their sentences, placing the words in the correct order.

"I'm done, Ms. Lesley," Rashaad says.

"Can you read me your sentence?" she asks him, leaning toward him as he reads his sentence to her.

"I am in the tree," he says.

"Great job!" Ms. Lesley exclaims. "Now, can you write your sentence?"

"Yes," Rashaad says confidently and writes his sentence on a piece of paper.

"Okay, here you go," Ms. Lesley says and places a sausage biscuit in front of Rashaad after he finishes writing. The biscuit is in a plastic wrapping, and it looks like the wrapper has been opened already. Rashaad looks at the biscuit skeptically.

"That's not the one that fell on the floor. It's a different one," Ms. Lesley clarifies.

Appearing satisfied with that explanation, Rashaad takes a bite of the biscuit. A big smile spreads across his face. "Thank you," he says.

"You're welcome," Ms. Lesley responds and turns her attention back to Amber. She asks Amber if she would like to read a book while Rashaad finishes his breakfast. "Yes, ma'am!" Amber says enthusiastically and chooses a book from a plastic bin Ms. Lesley places in front of her. Ms. Lesley listens to Amber read as Rashaad eats the first half of his sausage biscuit.

The balancing act that Ms. Lesley was trying to achieve—meeting a student's need for breakfast while still making sure that he received the scheduled reading instruction for the day—is a common challenge facing public school teachers in the United States. In 2013, more than half of all students in public schools were eligible for free and reduced-price meals—the first year that students living at or below 185 percent of the federal poverty line represented the majority of students in public schools.[2] According to a 2015 survey of public school teachers, administrators, and school support staff, three-quarters of teachers reported they see students regularly come to school hungry. And of these teachers, the vast majority (81 percent) said that they encounter a student who has come to school hungry at least once a week.[3]

During the first two decades of the twenty-first century, rising levels of income inequality in the United States, structural racism in housing and employment systems, and the Great Recession contributed to the increasing proportions of students and families living at or below the federal poverty level.[4] This book examines the work that schools and teachers do to respond to the social, emotional, and material needs of students in the context of long-standing racial and economic inequities and a set of school reform policies that sought to intervene in these inequities.

As public schools saw the proportion of students from economically disadvantaged families and communities increase, they also experienced increased pressure to improve the academic achievement of their students. Federal policies like the No Child Left Behind Act of 2001 (NCLB; reauthorized as the Every Student Succeeds Act in 2015) and the Race to the Top federal grant program required schools to demonstrate that they could increase the academic performance of their students, including the performance of economically disadvantaged students and students of color.

Meeting students' basic needs—ensuring they have access to nutritious meals and a sense of belonging and connection to school, for example—can positively influence students' academic performance.[5] In recognition of this, schools provide institutional supports in the form of school meals programs, school nurses, and school guidance counselors. However, these resources are not always available to students, whether due to low funding, lack of mandates, or competing priorities. When institutional supports have fallen short, individual teachers have often taken up this work, as Ms. Lesley did when she gave Rashaad the sausage biscuit. This book examines the types of work that individual teachers do to meet students' needs and how this work is influenced by school-level practices, government policy, and teachers' social locations.

When Ms. Lesley and I talked later that day, I recalled her interactions with Rashaad and asked Ms. Lesley about food she provides for students. Ms. Lesley shared some of the work she has done to provide food for students when school meals are not available and the personal and institutional factors that constrain this work. "I have provided food for students. I do it less than I used to," she explained. "I'm trying to draw more boundaries and not spend as much of my money when it's not really my job. But it's like when you have a hungry five year old . . . Like, he dropped his sandwich on the floor for breakfast. And that happened the other day, and it was someone else's fault. They asked a friend to open it, and the friend dropped it on the floor, and so I had a granola bar."

Ms. Lesley continued, describing other times she has provided food for students: "And one time, our cafeteria worker would not have a lunch ready for our kids when we were going on a field trip, and one of my kids just didn't have a lunch, and we were getting ready to leave. I had an extra Hot Pocket in my little freezer, so I heated that up for her and just took the hit because I'm like she needs to eat! You know? Like Rashaad dropped it because he was being reckless so I didn't give him a new one right away. But then he was really upset, and I could just see that if he didn't get food, he wasn't going to work. And to me, it's not worth it. And I don't want him to be hungry but I also want him to learn that he needs to be more careful. But, and I had gone in and took out a granola bar, and then I realized there was an extra [sausage biscuit] on the desk, so I gave him a sandwich instead from someone else's breakfast they didn't eat instead of my granola bar."

Ms. Lesley continues, describing additional factors that shape her work: "I mean, you have to be really careful because there are a lot of food allergies and issues these days but I always get all the information from parents ahead of time . . . We're also a healthy school and we're not supposed to provide food. We're not supposed to use food at all in here. But if I do have food, you know for a party or something, I have to get permission ahead of time, and it has to be healthy food, so I try to make healthier choices. And then other snacks for kids who are just hungry. I mean, they're five and they're hungry. I'm not going to let them sit there miserable. So, I just don't."

In our conversation, Ms. Lesley described the many different factors that influenced her decision to offer an additional breakfast to Rashaad. One was the desire to teach Rashaad to conserve resources in a context of limited resources, where each student was provided with one breakfast as part of the school's free breakfast program. Another was the knowledge that food was essential to academic learning and the desire for Rashaad to have the nutrition he needed to engage in the lesson. A third was Ms. Lesley's own context of limited resources in which she is trying to limit how much she spends on supplemental food for students. This leads to her relief at having a leftover breakfast item to substitute for the granola bar that she was planning to offer. As she decides what food to provide to students, Ms. Lesley also balances her awareness of individual students' food allergies and the requirements of the school's wellness policy that students be offered only healthy food. Ms. Lesley's work is further shaped by the ability of her school to provide food for students, such as the example of the cafeteria not being able to provide a school lunch for a student on a field trip day and the ways in which teachers' work is defined and rewarded in school reform policies (e.g., "it's not really my job").

This book is about the balancing act that schools and their teachers do to respond to the social, emotional, and material needs of their students and the contextual factors that shape and influence their responses, including the context of high-stakes accountability policies that strongly emphasize certain forms of academic learning. Several questions animate the analysis, including: What is the work that teachers do to meet students' social, emotional, and material needs? How is this work constrained and enabled by factors outside teachers' control such as school financing, school-level practices, and school reform policies (e.g., NCLB, Race to the Top, and the authorization of charter schools)? What are the implications of different forms of organizing how schools meet students' needs for the types of noncognitive skills that are taught in classrooms and the types of work that are required of teachers in different institutional settings?

School Reform Policies: No Child Left Behind, Achievement Gaps, and Charter Schools

In January 2001, three days after entering office, President George W. Bush introduced his framework for reforming public K-12 education in the United States, entitled No Child Left Behind. This collection of policy recommendations was designed to reduce academic achievement gaps among students of differing races, ethnicities, and socioeconomic statuses through the principles of accountability, choice, and flexibility.[6]

The passage of the NCLB in fall 2001 drew on these principles to make two significant changes to the U.S. K-12 public education system: first, it created a system of accountability for public schools based on high-stakes standardized testing and, second, it facilitated the development of school choice models, such as charter schools, that sought to provide students with choices beyond their neighborhood school.[7]

NCLB sought to create a market-based structure for public education in which schools would compete with each other for students based on their existing students' standardized test scores.[8] Within this system, as the market-based logic went, schools with higher standardized test scores would attract more students, while schools with lower test scores would lose students over time, and perhaps even "go out of business." Eventually, under this model, NCLB claimed that all students would have access to high quality schools, and achievement gaps would be eliminated. (NCLB initially had the goal of eliminating all achievement gaps by 2014.) While this market-based process played out, students attending consistently underperforming schools would have access to supplemental education programs, such as after school programs and private tutoring services, and the opportunity to transfer to a higher-performing school.[9]

NCLB institutionalized the use of standardized testing by requiring all states receiving federal education funding to test students in particular grades in reading, math, and science each year. The law also delineated how states would classify students' performance on these tests, directing states to use at least three performance levels (e.g., basic, proficient, and advanced). During the first decade of NCLB, schools were required to report whether they had made adequate yearly progress (AYP) each year, a classification created by NCLB to assess schools' progress in moving toward the goal of all students scoring proficient on the standardized tests by 2014. Schools that continuously failed to meet AYP faced a series of progressive sanctions, culminating in school closure and reconstitution.

The election of President Barack Obama in 2008 led to some changes in the structure of NCLB, offering more flexibility for schools while extending the reach of standardized testing to teacher evaluations. The Obama administration offered waivers of some of the NCLB's most punitive provisions to states who committed to creating new evaluation policies for teachers and administrators, adopting new curricular standards, and meeting goals for student growth in standardized test scores. The administration also reinforced these priorities through a competitive grant program, which incentivized the use of standardized test scores in teacher evaluations. The Race to the Top program provided $4.35 billion to states that committed to use "student growth" data—defined as standardized test scores for tested subjects and alternative assessments for non-tested subjects—in their evaluations of teachers' and administrators' work.[10]

Under Race to the Top, for the first time, public school teachers in many school districts across the nation would have up to half of their annual evaluations based on their students' performance on yearly standardized tests. A highly effective teacher, as defined by the Race to the Top grant solicitation, is one "whose students achieve high rates (e.g., one and one-half grade levels in an academic year) of student growth."[11] Race to the Top also incentivized the use of standards-based assessments, such as EdTPA, in teacher preparation programs and state certification requirements.[12] In incentivizing these practices, the Obama administration further institutionalized the use of standardized testing as a measure of schools' and, now, individual teachers' performance. Race to the Top also required applicants to describe how they would set standards for college and career readiness, leading many states to propose adopting the Common Core State Standards supported by the Obama administration.[13]

In 2015, President Obama institutionalized some of the flexibility that had been granted through waivers to NCLB by signing the Every Student Succeeds Act (ESSA), a reauthorization of NCLB. ESSA phased out the requirements that schools create annual measurable objectives based on a single standardized test and track annual yearly progress against those objectives. Instead, under ESSA, states are required to submit accountability plans and have flexibility in determining the goals of the accountability plans and the consequences for schools that do not meet accountability goals. ESSA still requires states to test students annually, but schools now have more flexibility over the content and timing of test administration. Similar to Race to the Top, the law requires states to set standards to measure students' progress in meeting college and career-readiness outcomes but does not mandate the adoption of Common Core Standards. Broadly, the law attempted to create more flexibility and fewer punitive consequences for schools in their efforts to close achievement gaps.

The research for this book was completed during the 2012–2013 and 2013–2014 school years, while schools were still subject to NCLB requirements but also beginning to gain flexibility through waivers, grapple with the implications of Race to the Top funding, and prepare for the adoption of Common Core standards. Because NCLB had not yet been reauthorized when the field work for this book was completed, the chapters that follow refer to the law as NCLB when discussing NCLB-related policies.

Alongside the system of standards-based accountability, a key element in the creation of a market-based structure for public education has been the authorization of charter schools. In a market-based model, proponents argue that charter schools provide increased choices for parents and students and increased competition for traditional public schools. Charter schools are privately managed and publicly funded educational institutions that are granted flexibility in how they operate with the requirement that they meet accountability standards set by a local education agency. Charter schools have permission to set their own school schedules, to develop unique curricular and cultural offerings, and to set their own hiring standards for teachers. (Individual charter schools operating within charter management organizations may have more limits on their organization.) In return, charter schools must demonstrate that their students can achieve at high levels academically, usually evaluated by their performance on standardized tests. A charter school that does not meet the requirements outlined in its charter can have its charter revoked.

As of June 2021, legislation to authorize the creation of charter schools had been passed in forty-five states in the United States and the District of Columbia. According to the National Center for Educational Statistics, from school year 2000–2001 to school year 2017–2018, the number of charter schools increased from 2,000 to 7,200 and the number of students attending charter schools increased from 0.4 million students to 3.1 million students. In school year 2017–2018, charter schools represented 7 percent of all public schools in the United States.[14]

Epple et al. reviewed empirical research on charter schools' academic outcomes and found mixed results, often depending on the methodology used to assess academic achievement and the types of charter schools included in the analyses.[15] In the absence of a consensus among charter school research studies, the authors offer an "interpretation that fits the evidence," namely, "that some charter schools, including especially the over-subscribed schools [charter schools that have more students who apply than they can accommodate], are in fact much more effective with respect to student achievement than their counterpart TPSs [traditional public schools], while the majority of charter schools are not superior, and some are inferior, to their counterpart TPSs."[16] The authors, among other scholars, also find that charter schools play a complicated role in school segregation. At the national level, charter schools enroll a higher percentage of Black and Hispanic students and students eligible for free and reduced-price meals than do traditional public schools.[17] Additionally, charter schools tend to have lower enrollments of special education students and English Language Learners than do traditional public schools located in the same neighborhoods.[18]

The charter school model was created prior to the implementation of NCLB and offered the promise of greater control over educational institutions by groups that historically had been marginalized from educational policies and practices. At the same time, charter schools also offered a way for more advantaged and affluent families to remove resources from traditional public schools. Wells et al. call this dynamic a "postmodern paradox" in which, in some cases, charter schools offer an opportunity for families, students, and educators of color to create institutions that empower and center the cultures and experiences of students of color while, in other cases, charter schools may contribute to a resegregation of resources in schools serving predominately White students.[19]

In the case of City Charter, the second school examined in this book, the school's diverse student body came as a result of processes of gentrification in the neighborhoods surrounding City Charter. The school was founded in the early 2000s as NCLB was first being implemented and during a period of rapid gentrification in the city where City Charter is located.[20] As increasing economic investment arrived in the neighborhoods throughout the city, racial and cultural displacement followed. The predominantly Black and working-class neighborhood where City Charter was founded was one of the neighborhoods significantly impacted by gentrification. Over a seven-year period, the median home values in the households closest to City Charter increased by over 40 percent. As home values increased, so did property taxes, making it more difficult for working-class homeowners to remain in the neighborhood.

The year before City Charter opened, the neighborhood's traditional public elementary school served fewer than 300 students, approximately three-quarters of whom identified as Black. Less than a decade later, the neighborhood school had been closed by the city government due to low enrollment and what the city defined as low performance, as measured primarily by students' scores on standardized tests. Media coverage of gentrification in the neighborhood pointed to the opening of charter schools, including City Charter, as one element contributing to the process of gentrification. As more White families moved to the neighborhood during this period, they were more likely to send their students to City Charter than to the neighborhood public school. During the year that I observed, City Charter served a student population that was 43 percent Black/African American, 17 percent White, and 32 percent

Latino/Hispanic. More than half (60 percent) of students were eligible for free and reduced-price meals.

In Ms. Kelly's first grade classroom, Rachel, a student whom I perceived to be Black and female, enters the room holding a smart phone in one hand. She is with an adult whom I perceive to be Black and male and who looks to me like he might be in his late twenties or early thirties. He is holding a tray of the school breakfast in one hand. With his other hand, he hangs up Rachel's backpack in her cubby. He encourages Rachel to sit down and eat her breakfast, and Rachel sits down at a round table by the cubbies where the students store their belongings. "Eat your food and don't be disrespectful. Be quiet when Ms. Kelly says it's quiet time, and don't eat with your mouth open. Okay! I love you," the man says to Rachel. He starts to walk toward the classroom door, and Rachel looks after him and smiles.

"Bryan, if you're going to sleep, go ahead. If not, I'm going to take you downstairs soon," Ms. Kelly says to one of her students. Ms. Kelly who identifies as White and female, has been teaching first grade at City Charter for five years. Bryan, a student whom I perceived to be Black and male, walks to a desk at the front of the carpet and takes out red, noise-cancelling headphones from inside the desk. He walks back to the classroom library and curls up on a beanbag chair.

"20 minus 17," says Ms. Kelly. "3," say the students.

"20 minus 18," says Ms. Kelly. "2," say the students.

"20 minus 19," says Ms. Kelly. "1," say the students.

"20 minus 20," says Ms. Kelly. "Zeeeero," say the students.

Ms. Kelly picks a popsicle stick out of a black plastic cup. "Lori," she says. "Yay!" Lori replies as she moves to the front of the carpet to lead the other students in correcting the spelling, punctuation, and capitalization of a passage Ms. Kelly has written on the white board. "You are the teacher," Ms. Kelly says to her.

Lori, whom I perceive to be White and female, is a commanding presence at the front of the carpet. She stands on the cubby shelf with her back to the white board and tells a fellow student to sit on her bottom. Lori asks Ms. Kelly for the plastic cup of popsicle sticks. She picks out one of the sticks and calls on a student whom I perceive to be Latino and male. He pauses. "You can skip if you want to," Lori tells him but he declines. "Do you want me to come back?" she asks, and he indicates that he does.

Lori picks another popsicle stick. "Tamara, take a break," Lori says to a student whom I perceive to be Black and female and who is talking, using the school's term for a "timeout." "Ooooh," several students say. Ms. Kelly looks like she is trying to suppress a smile. "She's the teacher now," Ms. Kelly tells the students. Tamara gets up and sits at a table next to the carpet. She returns to the carpet about a minute later. "Bryan," Lori calls out. "He's taking a nap,"

Jamie, a student whom I perceive to be White and female, responds. "That's the first time he's slept," Ms. Kelly whispers to me.

At City Charter, the school had institutionalized a curriculum that integrated academic, social, and emotional learning and granted teachers ample resources and latitude with which to meet students' basic needs within the boundaries of the school day. One of these resources was the school's extended day, which allowed more time for students' needs to be met, in this case, extra time for Rachel to eat breakfast and for Bryan to take a nap. The school's approach to social and emotional learning, which included the Responsive Classroom approach,[21] emphasized students practicing communicating with peers and adults, as Lori did when she led the class in the editing activity. The conditions of learning at City Charter that allowed for this type of integration were very different than those of Oak Grove Elementary School and they point to larger patterns of inequalities that exist between schools.

One area of inequality was in the amount of resources that each institution was able to mobilize. City Charter School was proposed and founded with financial support from a private nonprofit organization that was interested in developing school reform models that could be scaled-up and implemented across the United States. The private nonprofit provided funding for the planning of City Charter and helped to fund the rental of the first space that housed the school. Connections to school reform networks and private foundations allowed the school to grow its enrollment and staffing and to provide an extended school day and school year to students. In turn, the extended school day and school year and the presence of a large number of school staff members supported the school's approach to integrating academic, social, and emotional learning.

Most classrooms I observed at City Charter had two to three adults working with children at a time, and the school employed a full-time nurse, social worker, and culture coordinator to support students' social, emotional, and physical health. At the time that I observed at City Charter, the base per pupil funding amount that the school received from the city budget was over $10,000, and the school regularly raised millions of dollars a year in additional support from private sources.

The wealth that City Charter was able to mobilize on its students' behalf is not characteristic of all charter schools in its city or the United States and is not limited to charter schools. Traditional public schools in wealthier communities have raised private funds to support the operations of their school. What is notable about the resources that City Charter was able to mobilize is that the school was able to leverage its connections to a network of private funders associated with the school reform movement and the early recognition it gained as a "high-performing" school. In its first five years of operation, City Charter became known as a highly performing school based on its students' performance on standardized assessments, compared to students in other charter schools in the city.

In the years following the celebration of City Charter as one of the highest performing charter schools in its jurisdiction, City Charter remained highly regarded even though its test scores no longer placed it in the highest level of school performance. Thus, it appeared that school reform policies gave City Charter access both to a network of financial resources and to a status that helped it to continue to leverage these resources. The school's status as an independent charter school (not part of a larger charter school network) and as a high-performing school meant that it was not subject to the amount or intensity of surveillance directed toward traditional public schools, like Oak Grove, that were labeled "low-performing." These factors point to the role of school reform policies in shaping the types of resources that schools are able to mobilize on students' behalf.

"Pulling Apart?": School Reform and Economic Inequalities in the United States

Over the past decade, school reform policies have been implemented during a time of widening income inequality in the United States and during one of the worst recessions in the nation's history.[22] As schools and their teachers are confronted with school reform requirements to close academic achievement gaps, they are also met with the challenge of teaching students who live in a country where access to adequate housing and enough food to eat are not guaranteed and where access has been racially patterned due to individual-level and structural forms of racism.

Ms. Lesley teaches at Oak Grove Elementary, a traditional public school located in a suburb of a city in the mid-Atlantic region of the United States. The school's one-story brick building is surrounded by trees and nestled in a community of garden-style apartments. The apartments surrounding Oak Grove Elementary were built in the 1960s but the larger community of Oak Grove was established three decades earlier, during the Great Depression. Oak Grove was a public works project funded by the federal government to provide jobs and affordable housing during a time of economic scarcity. Both Black and White workers built the first housing in Oak Grove, and the original plans for the community included separate sections of the community where Black and White families could apply for residency. However, during the construction of Oak Grove, the federal government reneged on its commitment to include housing for Black families and restricted applications to White households who could demonstrate that they were married, the male applicant was employed, and the household earned between a certain minimum and maximum amount of income per year.

For the next quarter of a century, Oak Grove remained a segregated community, not unlike other suburban communities throughout the United States where the practices of redlining and restrictive covenants limited access to homeownership to White individuals. In the 1960s, increased transportation and real estate development combined with successful social movements for fair housing practices, led to the desegregation of the larger Oak Grove community. During this time, developers built the garden-style apartments surrounding Oak Grove Elementary, and the county built an elementary school to serve the new development. The garden-style apartments in the new development included affordable housing that, thirty years after the original community of Oak Grove was built, was now accessible to Black households and other households of color.

By 2012, the two Census tracts surrounding Oak Grove Elementary were home to more than 6,000 residents. Nearly half of all residents identified as Black/African American, about three in ten identified as White, and close to 10 percent identified as Asian. About 14 percent identified as Hispanic/Latino. While Oak Grove had become more racially and ethnically diverse, none of the housing built in the neighborhoods closest to Oak Grove Elementary was owner-occupied, meaning that the increased access to Oak Grove that households of color were able to achieve in these particular neighborhoods was not accompanied by the wealth-building benefits of homeownership. The rental housing was largely considered affordable and accessible to families with limited incomes; however, families would have to move outside the neighborhoods immediately surrounding Oak Grove to own housing.

The historical and structural inequities that were built into the creation of Oak Grove Elementary continue to shape the resources that the school has available to meet students' needs and serve as a reminder that "low-income schools" are not naturally occurring. During the school year that I observed at Oak Grove (2013–2014), 85 percent of students at the school were eligible for free and reduced-price school meals. More than half the students identified as Hispanic/Latino and over 40 percent identified as Black/African American. To be eligible for reduced-price meals, a family needs to have an annual household income no greater than 185 percent of the federal poverty line, which was $35,317 for a family of three during the year I observed at Oak Grove. To be eligible for free meals, a family is required to have an annual household income of no greater than 130 percent of the federal poverty line, which was $24,817 for a family of three.[23] Both of these levels of household income are far below what researchers estimate a family of three needs to get by in a high-cost-of-living region like the one in which Oak Grove is located.

The difficulties that families face making ends meet in a region with such a high cost of living are often exacerbated during times of economic crisis. The research for this book was completed in 2012 and 2013, in the aftermath of the Great Recession. During the Great Recession (December 2007 to June 2009), nearly 7.5 million jobs were lost, the most significant period of job loss since World War II. The recession also contributed to a significant increase in the number of people living in poverty, from 39.8 million in 2008 to 43.6 million in 2009, the largest number of individuals living in poverty documented in the fifty-one years that poverty estimates have been published.[24]

During the year that I completed observations at Oak Grove Elementary, two research centers published a report called "Pulling Apart," which detailed the Great Recession's effect on already significant levels of income inequality in the United States.[25] The report noted that while households at all income levels had lost income during the Great Recession, the incomes of the wealthiest households had begun to grow again in the first few years post-recession, while the incomes of lower- and middle-income families were slow to recover. This meant that many families sending their children to Oak Grove Elementary and schools throughout the country were likely still experiencing the effects of the recession three or more years after it had officially ended. For some families, the economic recession may have made it even more difficult to find employment and for others it may have meant falling below the official poverty line.

At the same time that students and their families were experiencing economic challenges due to the recession and long-standing inequities in housing, education, and employment systems, the funding provided to schools like Oak Grove was not keeping pace with increasing academic demands and increasing student needs. A report commissioned by the state in which Oak Grove was located to examine funding levels for schools recommended an increase in the base level of funding per student from the current level of approximately $6,900 per student to approximately $10,900 per student. The report called for the increase to support both academic-related aims (e.g., teacher professional development, smaller class sizes, additional instructional staff) and resources to meet students' social, emotional, and material needs (e.g., school counselors, school nurses, and school social workers).

As those who participated in the state study recognized, without adequate resources to meet basic needs, such as healthy food, safe housing, and access to quality health care, it is difficult for students to meet their academic potential. In a study comparing the cognitive performance of kindergartners, those who had experienced at least one characteristic of food insecurity had poorer performance on a fall math assessment and less learning growth in math throughout the school year than students who did not experience any food insecurity.[26] Children ages six to eleven who reported that their family sometimes or often did not have enough food to eat were significantly more likely to have lower math scores, to have repeated a grade, and to have trouble getting along with other children.[27] Older children who experienced food insufficiency in their homes were more likely to have been suspended from school and to have had difficulty interacting with other students.[28]

Just as access to food matters to learning, so does access to health care and housing. Students who lack the ability to visit the dentist or eye doctor tend to have lower school attendance and academic performance.[29] Students who move frequently to find adequate or affordable housing are likely to have lower academic test scores than their peers with access to more housing stability.[30] The studies cited here are part of a larger body of research that demonstrates a significant cost of inequitable access to well-paying employment, housing, and food: the ability of students to engage to their fullest potential in school.

How Schools Respond to Students' Needs

From the nineteenth century, in the absence of stronger social welfare policies, schools have played a role in meeting students' basic needs. Schools have provided food for students and, in some cases, access to school health professionals, such as nurses and counselors. In doing so, many schools have struggled with limited resources to meet students' social, emotional, and material needs and have reproduced inequities as they attempted to meet those needs.

In the nineteenth century, volunteers provided free meals in school to children from economically disadvantaged households. The federal government first established a school lunch program during the Great Depression and institutionalized the program in 1946, with the passage of the National School Lunch Act. Two decades later, the federal government piloted a School Breakfast Program as part of the Child Nutrition Act of 1966. Both programs continue to provide reimbursements to schools to fund free and reduced-cost meals for students.

More recently, programs and policies have sought to make school meals more accessible to students. To address low participation in school breakfast programs, schools have implemented Universal School Breakfast Programs and Breakfast in the Classroom Programs.[31] Universal School Breakfast Programs provide breakfast free of charge to all students in an effort to reduce the stigma that can exist when the program is limited to students whose families earn 130 percent or less of the federal poverty line. Breakfast in the Classroom Programs offer grab-and-go breakfast items for students to eat in their classrooms, eliminating the need for students to arrive early to school to eat breakfast. In 2010, the Healthy Hunger-Freed Kids Act authorized the Community Eligibility Provision (CEP), which allows schools with at least 40 percent of students eligible for free meals to provide free school breakfast and lunch to all students, regardless of their economic status.[32] Research on universal meals, including the CEP, has found that schools that have increased access to school meals have seen significant increases in student meal participation and promising outcomes related to student health, discipline, and grade promotion.[33]

In addition to feeding students, schools often provide physical and mental health services via school nurses, guidance counselors, and social workers. Schools may also implement particular programming oriented to meeting students' social and emotional needs, as City Charter did with its adoption of the Responsive Classroom approach. Schools may also provide resources to meet students' material needs. At Oak Grove Elementary, the school provided clothing to students who needed winter jackets and served as the site for a free produce distribution to families once a week after school.[34]

While schools continue to play an important role in meeting students' needs, they have been constrained by limited resources and have at times reproduced the inequities that they were trying to address. Federal law now requires all schools receiving federal funding to provide free or reduced-price lunches to eligible students; however, there is no similar federal law requiring access to school breakfast, school nurses, social workers, or guidance counselors. Only half of the states in the United States mandate school counseling for students in both primary and secondary schools.[35] During the 2015–2016 school year, slightly more than half of public schools employed a full-time school nurse, meaning that the remainder had intermittent (part-time) access to a school nurse or no access at all.[36]

In the case of the School Lunch Program, for many decades, school meals programs discriminated against students who could not pay for meals, in practice, if not in law. Some school districts denied access to school meals to students whose families received cash assistance, while other districts allowed school officials discretion to determine who would receive food.[37] In some districts, school officials offered different amounts and quality of food to students who paid for school lunch versus students who received free meals.[38] In the 1960s, the NAACP Legal Defense Fund and the Black Panther Party raised awareness about the lack of access and discrimination in school feeding programs and, in the case of the Black Panther Party, established their own highly successful school breakfast programs.[39] While discrimination in school feeding programs has led to ongoing stigma related to receiving free meals, current policies such as Breakfast in the Classroom and Universal School Meals Programs seek to make free meals widely accessible to all students, particularly in schools with high percentages of students eligible for free and reduced-price meals.

In the absence of stronger mandates and additional funding, students in the United States can encounter a very different set of resources, depending on the school they attend (and in the case of neighborhood schools, depending on the neighborhood they live in). This book examines school-level practices to meet students' needs and how efforts to do so are both shaped by extra-local factors and implicated in processes of social reproduction.

This Study

The fieldwork for this study, which includes classroom observations and interviews, focused on the experiences of elementary school teachers working at two schools, City Charter School and Oak Grove Elementary, during the final years of NCLB implementation and the transition to Obama-era school reform policies, such as Race to the Top. It draws on methods of inquiry associated with institutional ethnography, first articulated by Dorothy Smith.[40] Institutional ethnography provides a way to explore the social organization of inequalities without abstracting them from the daily lived experiences of the people who are affected by them. It begins from the actual experiences of people, building an account of their daily activities, and then moves beyond these local activities to map the extra-local social relations, embedded in policies, practices, and institutions, that help to structure individuals' daily lives.

Adopting methods of inquiry associated with institutional ethnography allowed me to examine the everyday work that teachers engaged in to meet students' social, emotional, and material needs. It also allowed me to begin to map the many extra-local contextual factors that shaped and structured teachers' work, including school reform policies, school funding, and school-wide practices, and the ways in which these extra-local factors were intertwined. Drawing on theories of social and cultural reproduction, I also examined the ways in which these extra-local factors shape the conditions of learning in the two schools, with implications for the types of noncognitive skills and forms of cultural capital that are emphasized in schools.

My work began by documenting teachers' work in schools at the classroom level. I sought to capture the many different dimensions of teachers' work to meet students' social, emotional, and material needs. I also sought to understand the many factors that influence this work, including school-level practices and school reform policies. I brought with me a curiosity and a critical perspective on this work from the year I worked as a Teach For America (TFA) teacher in a rural school district in Mississippi. In spite of what I had learned during my TFA training about the importance of focusing on academic outcomes, it was clear to me over the course of that year that the students who I worked with and I could engage in learning together more deeply and meaningfully when we'd had enough food to eat, enough sleep at night, and felt connected to each other.

As a White woman teaching Black students in a segregated school system, that year also required me to start to understand the multilevel factors that shaped my interactions with students in the classroom, including the history of racism and racial violence in Mississippi, ongoing patterns of racial and economic segregation in public schooling, low levels of resources provided to public schools, and the role of school reform policies in allowing me to teach without a traditional teaching credential and in imposing pressures on our school to improve test scores under the threat of school closure. I also started to become aware of the limitations I brought to the classroom in my lack of understanding and incorporation of the many cultural strengths and assets students brought to the classroom.

As my first year of teaching came to a close, I recognized that these contextual factors were expressed in a particular way locally in the community where I taught but were also present in the community where I was returning to live, over 2,000 miles away. With this project, I was curious to explore teachers' work in a different region of the United States to see how they approached the work of meeting students' needs and how this work was enabled and constrained by school-level practices, government policy, and teachers' social locations.

My work began by finding schools to partner with for this research. As a teacher in Mississippi, I could observe my work and my interactions with my students without formal approval. As a dissertation student, I attempted to gain access to schools in a more formalized way. This proved to be very difficult, especially for conducting research in traditional public schools. To be able to observe in a traditional public school as a researcher, I first had to receive two levels of approval for my research—one from the Institutional Review Board (IRB) at my university and one from the IRB of the school district. I understood from talking to others who had tried to conduct research in public schools that my application would be more likely to be approved if I did not include students as subjects of my research. (To do so would require an additional level of scrutiny from the IRBs and would likely require me to obtain parental consent from each of the students in the study in order for them to participate.)

Since teachers were the main focus of my research, I pursued my application focusing solely on teachers. This decision created some significant limitations in being able to accurately characterize students' racial, ethnic, and gender identities, which I discuss in more detail below. After many unsuccessful applications to school districts, including the school district in the central city where City Charter was located, I was very fortunate to be permitted to research in Oak Grove's district. A friend of a friend who taught at Oak Grove helped me to secure her principal's permission to do research and walked me around the school one day after school to recruit teachers for the study. Lead teachers in five classrooms agreed to participate in the study.

While I pursued approval from public school districts, a friend also connected me with her colleague who taught in a charter school in the central city. Charter schools were given autonomy from the IRB requirements of their school district so a meeting with an administrator, a volunteer form, and a background check later, I was approved to research at City Charter. The administrator sent an email to City Charter teachers, and lead teachers in four classrooms agreed to allow me to observe.

Observing Teachers' Work

I continue to be grateful to the fifteen teachers at City Charter and Oak Grove who welcomed me into their classrooms and allowed me to jot field notes while they worked. I wanted to document in as much detail as possible teachers' actions and interactions with students and so I generally chose a place at the periphery of the classroom to sit and jot notes. I generally observed the entire day in teachers' classrooms, from when students arrived for breakfast in the morning to when they left school in the afternoon. I spent between two and three months at each school, conducting twenty-one classroom observations and ten interviews at City Charter from March through May 2013 and twenty classroom observations and nine interviews at Oak Grove Elementary from December 2013 through February 2014. While my time at both schools was limited by the level of access I was able to gain, I did reach a point where I saw similar patterns of interaction repeated, particularly as they related to the significant standardized testing requirements at Oak Grove Elementary and the way in which social and emotional learning and restorative practices were implemented at City Charter School.

At City Charter School, five lead teachers and three assistant teachers who taught first through third graders agreed to participate in the study. Two of the lead teachers co-taught a single classroom, so I observed four classrooms at City Charter School. At Oak Grove Elementary, seven lead teachers, who taught kindergarteners through third graders, agreed to participate in the study. Two of the lead teachers at Oak Grove also co-taught a single classroom, so the total number of classrooms observed at Oak Grove was six.

I completed half and full-day observations of teachers' work in their classrooms, visiting teachers' classrooms multiple times over the course of the observation period. During these observations, I documented teachers' daily activities in their classrooms, paying particular attention to teachers' work and how it was shaped and influenced by school reform policies. These daily activities included whole class instruction, meetings with small groups of students, supervision of students' breakfast and lunch time, and meetings with colleagues. I also observed informal interactions between teachers and parents (e.g., parents stopping by unscheduled to speak with teachers before or after school or parents dropping off or picking up their students from school) but did not attend formal parent meetings or conferences.

Toward the end of the observation period, I also asked teachers for permission to interview them about their work. The semi-structured interviews were designed to collect information about what motivates teachers to teach, the work they perform inside and outside of the school day, and their perceptions of this work. During the interviews, I also asked teachers to reflect on particular instances of student challenges or the influence of school reform policies that I observed in the classroom. I supplemented these interviews with conversations with administrators and school support staff. Pseudonyms are used for all teachers, students, and schools in this study.

After each interview, the participants completed a brief demographic questionnaire, based on the National Schools and Staffing Survey. All but one of the nineteen interview participants were female, and the male participant was an administrator at Oak Grove Elementary. The sample of teachers I interviewed at Oak Grove was more racially and ethnically diverse than the sample of teachers I interviewed at City Charter. Teachers interviewed at Oak Grove were also more likely to be older, to have more years of teaching experience, and less likely to be alternatively certified than teachers at City Charter. (The Appendix provides more information about teachers' demographic characteristics at each school.)

While I surveyed teachers about their racial, ethnic, and gender identities, I did not do the same for the students in the classrooms I observed. This was a pragmatic decision made in an attempt to ease IRB approval but it provided significant limitations in terms of accurately describing students' racial, ethnic, and gender identities. In the absence of gathering information directly from students, I used a combination of my own observations and information I learned from listening to conversations among students and teachers to describe students' social locations in this book. In effect these are my best guesses about students' possible racial, ethnic, and gender identities based on pronouns that students used to describe themselves and others, information students shared about their race, ethnicity, and/or country of origin, and ways that teachers classified students' social locations. Where I was unable to or did not collect this information when describing a particular interaction, I have simply used the word "student." However, since race, ethnicity, and gender play a large role in shaping our social interactions, I have tried to provide as much descriptive information as possible about students' social locations, with the very real possibility that I may be mis-gendering students who did not feel safe in correcting a peer or adult's misuse of a personal pronoun or inaccurately describing a student's race or ethnicity. When describing students, I frequently use language such as "who I perceived to be female and Latina" to remind the reader that these are my perceptions and not students' preferred ways of describing their identities.

In this study, Oak Grove Elementary and City Charter School are not meant to be representative of all traditional public schools and charter schools respectively. Nor are they meant to be directly comparable to each other. What these two schools do illuminate is how factors external to the classroom shape social interactions among teachers and students during a particularly significant period of school reform policy, the consequences of these factors for how schools meet students' needs, and the implications of these on the processes of social reproduction at each school.

As the chapters that follow will demonstrate, school reform policies contributed to very different levels and types of autonomy at the two schools in this study. For example, teachers' work at Oak Grove Elementary was subject to a different level of scrutiny from outside observers under prevailing school reform policies than was teachers' work at City Charter. Teachers at Oak Grove

Elementary were frequently required to provide tangible evidence of their and their students' achievement to satisfy federal and school district requirements and had less flexibility over how these assessments were scheduled and implemented. The audit culture that shaped teachers' work at Oak Grove Elementary also had implications for how teachers interacted with students and processes of social and cultural reproduction at the school.

Conversely, teachers at City Charter had fewer external constraints imposed on their work due to the flexibility given to charter schools and the positive regard that City Charter was granted as an institution. However, teachers faced internal constraints to their autonomy related to the school's culture of urgency around closing achievement gaps, closely tied to social movement aspects of school reform.[41] The dominant culture of social and emotional learning and restorative disciplinary practices also shaped the way that teachers interacted with students at City Charter, with an emphasis on reproducing aspects of White middle-class culture.

In addition to examining how school reform policies influence teachers' work, this book also examines the ways that teachers' work in the context of school reform policies may influence processes of social and cultural reproduction in their schools. The constraints that school reform policies place on teachers' work also constrain teachers' relationships with their students and, in some cases, the abilities of teachers to offer culturally relevant and affirming alternatives to the dominant culture of education. In this way, school reform policies may be frustrating the very aims they claim to espouse—reducing educational inequalities and promoting high levels of academic achievement among students of color.

The Chapters that Follow

Chapter 1 details the types of work that teachers do to meet students' social, emotional, and material needs at Oak Grove Elementary and City Charter School. Education reform policies, such as NCLB and Race to the Top, attempt to reduce the ambiguity inherent in teachers' work by quantifying teaching outputs as students' performance on standardized tests, a practice that is part of a larger process of rationalization in teachers' work. Defining teachers' work so narrowly misses the important aspects of teachers' work that is not so easily measured, including the relational work that teachers engage in with their students and their attempts to meet students' social, emotional, and material needs. This chapter seeks to reclaim and make visible these aspects of teachers' work through an analysis of interviews with teachers at Oak Grove Elementary and City Charter and through observations of teachers' work in their classrooms.

The next two chapters focus on school reform and teachers' work at Oak Grove Elementary. Chapter 2 examines the ways that high-stakes testing and standards-based accountability policies, such as NCLB and Race to the Top, influence the culture of teachers' work at the school level. I find that an audit culture pervades the way that teachers' work is organized at Oak Grove, with frequent surveillance of teachers' work from school officials inside and outside the school and numerous requirements for teachers to document the outcomes they and their students were achieving in the classroom. In some cases, this audit culture also extended into teachers' interactions with colleagues when grade-level meetings were required to be documented for external review. This chapter also explores the ways that teachers cognitively distance themselves from school reform requirements that do not seem relevant to the practice of teaching and teachers' own internalized notions of accountability, which include tailoring lessons to meet the individual needs of their students and helping to address opportunity gaps that students face, whether by providing access to food or reaching out to students' families to better understand challenges that students are facing at home.

Chapter 3 examines how the audit culture that influences teachers' work shapes interactions between students and teachers at Oak Grove Elementary. An analysis of observations of teachers' work at Oak Grove demonstrates that the frequent requirement to test students to meet school reform mandates results in an emphasis on a particular set of noncognitive skills, particularly the skills of following routines and directions, working quietly and independently, and limiting autonomy. It then compares these characteristics to Anyon's typology, demonstrating that the curriculum of standardized testing corresponds closely to the skills and knowledge associated with working-class employment, suggesting a role for standardized testing in a process of social reproduction at the school.[42] The chapter then contrasts two mornings in Ms. Jackson's classroom to demonstrate that the work that Ms. Jackson is doing on a "normal" morning in her classroom includes the transmission of a broader array of noncognitive skills, including elements of culturally responsive teaching and culturally relevant pedagogy. This is contrasted with the much narrower set of noncognitive skills transmitted during a standardized testing day.

The next two chapters focus on school reform and teachers' work at City Charter School. Chapter 4 explores the way that school reform as a social movement to reduce achievement gaps among Black, Latino and White students shapes teachers' work at the school level. The chapter explores how a sense of urgency that has been identified as a characteristic of school reform movements[43] combined with a culture of individual responsibility and a lack of unionization at the school contributes to overwork and burnout among teachers.

Chapter 5 examines how the school's commitment to restorative practices shapes interactions between teachers and students at City Charter. An analysis of observations of teachers' interactions with their students shows that teachers enacted a common set of practices oriented to increasing students' noncognitive skills, including a facility and ease in speaking to adults and peers, an ability to self-regulate and manage work independently that goes beyond the following of a routine and delineated set of tasks, and an ability to negotiate and solve conflicts peacefully. These skills and interactional strategies closely align with the evaluative standards of middle-class institutions and, as a result, potentially prepare students to engage with educational institutions that adopt this dominant culture with more ease.

However, missing from City Charter's approach was an engagement with students' cultures and the nondominant forms of capital they brought to the classroom. While teachers provided opportunities for students to share information about their weekend or to bring in an object to share with other students in the class as part of morning meeting, a reciprocal exchange of learning seemed missing from these interactions. Providing more opportunities for students to share their own skills and assets as part of these interactions could have made cultural learning at City Charter travel both ways, from teacher to student and from student to teacher.

Part 1

The Work of Teaching

• •

1

Beyond Standardized Testing

• •

Meeting Students' Social, Emotional, and Material Needs

On a rainy spring afternoon at City Charter, Ms. Kelly, a first grade teacher who identifies as White and female, is sitting behind a crescent-shaped table at the back of her classroom. On the back wall of her classroom there are two large windows that, on sunny days, let lots of natural light into the classroom. There is a classroom library in one of the back corners where six students are clustered, each working on a packet of worksheets. Other students are spread across the classroom, some sitting at the tables in the center of the room and others sprawled out on the large carpet at the front of the room.

Ms. Kelly calls several students over to the table to work with her on a math assignment.

"Lori, you look a little bit upset. Do you want to get some water?" Ms. Kelly asks. Lori, a student with short curly brown hair who is wearing a sleeveless loose leopard print patterned dress and who I perceived to be White and female, gets up and leaves the classroom. "Is she sad or hurt or both?" Ms. Kelly asks Serena, a small girl who I perceived to be Latina and female, her wavy brown hair pulled back into a ponytail. Serena says something quietly. "A little bit of both," Ms. Kelly confirms.

Throughout the school day at both City Charter and Oak Grove Elementary, teachers inquired about and sought to meet students' needs, including needs that were both beyond the scope of academic learning and directly supported it. This chapter examines the many ways in which teachers sought to meet students' social, emotional, and material needs and the factors that constrained and enabled teachers' efforts at each school. By examining the types of work that teachers engaged in to meet students' needs, we can better understand the multidimensionality of teachers' work and regain an understanding of the complexity of this work, even as school reform policies narrowly define what type of labor "counts."

Education reform policies, such as No Child Left Behind (NCLB) and Race to the Top, attempt to reduce the ambiguity inherent in teachers' work by quantifying teaching "outputs" as students' performance on standardized tests, a practice that is part of a larger process of rationalization in teachers' work. Defining teachers' work so narrowly misses the important aspects of teachers' work that is not so easily measured, including the relational work that teachers engage in with their students and their attempts to meet students' social, emotional, and material needs. This chapter seeks to reclaim and make visible these aspects of teachers' work through an analysis of interviews with teachers at Oak Grove Elementary and City Charter and through observations of teachers' work in their classrooms.

In *Caring Democracy*, Joan Tronto describes care work as a series of nested practices in which some caring practices rely on other caring practices in order to succeed.[1] Tronto gives the example of a health-care organization; if this organization provides a doctor but not medical equipment, the organization has not succeeded in providing an adequate level of medical care. Thus, the caring actions of the doctor rely on the actions of those who manufacture, deliver, and clean this equipment. The coordination of these activities within a particular institutional context is critical for the adequate provision of medical care. In the same way, schools' efforts to promote the academic achievement of their students rely on practices that respond to students' social, emotional, and material needs. Tronto's conceptualization of "nested practices" invites us to consider whether schools will be able to achieve school reform goals without the reproductive labor that provides students with food to eat and a sense of connection and belonging during the school day.

Feeding Students

On a cold December morning, I park my car across from a bus stop about a block away from Oak Grove Elementary School. It's a few minutes before 7:45 A.M. I walk quickly toward the school, trying to make it there before the late bell rings and the custodian locks the entrance to the school. As I get closer to the large, one-story tan brick building, I hear a voice calling out, "last call for breakfast." A tall adult wearing a long gray peacoat, who I perceived to be Black and female, her dark hair gathered under a hat, is encouraging several children to hurry so that they will not miss the school breakfast. "I'm starting to walk backwards," she says and begins to slowly make her way back to the school's doorway with the school breakfast tickets. A small child wearing a thick winter jacket and dark pants, who I perceived to be male and Latino, falls in his rush to make it to the door. A few students stop to see if he is okay and the student stands up, appearing to be unharmed.

Near the entrance to the school, an adult wearing a bright pink zip-up sweatshirt with dark hair gathered into a long ponytail, who I perceived to be female and Latina, leans down to give a child one more kiss. "You have to let her go so she can get breakfast," the woman with the breakfast tickets advises the woman in the pink sweatshirt. I follow a few students into the school and stop by the front office to sign in.

As I cross the lobby a few minutes later, I hear the school custodian telling the arriving students that they have missed the school breakfast and need to go directly to their classrooms. The late bell has already rung and the clock in the hallway reads 7:48 A.M. The custodian repeats the message about breakfast being over again as each new group of students enters the school.

I continue down a hallway to Ms. Robinson's third grade classroom. Students are standing in a line at the front of the room with packets of papers in their hands, waiting for Ms. Robinson to check their homework. The remainder of the students are at their desks, talking and/or eating the school breakfast.

Shortly before I began observing at the school, Oak Grove Elementary had been selected as one of several elementary schools in its district to participate in a nationwide Breakfast in the Classroom program. Funded by a private grant, the program enabled students who arrived to school on time to pick up an individual bag of breakfast from the cafeteria free of charge to eat in their classroom. Studies of school breakfast programs have found that students who participate in these programs tend to perform better on tests of cognitive development than do students who do not participate in the program.[2] The programs have also been shown to reduce rates of absenteeism in schools.[3] However, participation in school breakfast programs is much lower than participation in school lunch programs. One study estimates that less than half of all students eligible for free and reduced breakfast participate in the program on an average day.[4]

To combat low participation, some schools have experimented with Universal School Breakfast Programs and Breakfast in the Classroom Programs, both of which have been demonstrated to increase school breakfast participation.[5] Universal School Breakfast Programs make free breakfast available to all students in an effort to reduce stigma that students accessing school breakfast can encounter when the program is associated with economic status. Breakfast in the Classroom Programs offer a la carte breakfast options for students to take with them to eat in their classrooms during the school day, eliminating the requirement for students to arrive early to school to eat breakfast.

At Oak Grove Elementary, school breakfast was a regular part of the school day, included on each classroom teacher's morning schedule and accessed by many students at the school. In the mornings, there frequently was a long line of students in the cafeteria waiting to pick up their breakfast. The school breakfast was often packaged in a way that appeared to be designed to appeal to students; students received their breakfast in a paper bag that looked similar to a McDonald's fast food bag. In the five classrooms I observed, anywhere from half to nearly all of the students who had arrived at school early or on time were eating school breakfast. However, once the school day started, students who arrived late to school often were not able to access breakfast. In these cases, individual teachers helped to fill in the gaps.

Ms. Robinson, who identifies as Black and female, is in her fifth year of teaching overall and fourth year of teaching at Oak Grove Elementary. Ms. Robinson immigrated to the United States when she was a child and began teaching out of a desire to support students' educational and social development. "I started teaching Sunday school, first. So, like me kind of just working with those kids in Sunday school . . . they were telling me all kinds of crazy stories about what would happen at school. I was like, 'Oh wow, well maybe I can help some of these students in the school system outside of the church.' And then also, I'm a part of an organization that contributed money to build an elementary school in [my home country] . . . And then I guess it all kind of ties in with what I did in college with international studies. I, my whole take on you know globalization, everything, was that um that in order to develop a people, to me, it has to start with education," she explained.

To address the challenge of students arriving late and missing breakfast, Ms. Robinson organized a system of mutual aid in her classroom, where students who had breakfast items they did not want to eat saved them for students who arrived late to school. "Whenever they don't want something, I have them put it up there at the front," Ms. Robinson shared. "There's a blue tray up there that they manage—any milk that they don't want, any food that they don't want, fruit, whatever, and I'll just leave it here up until about specials in case someone comes in and they're absolutely hungry. They have that because I know that the cafeteria won't open the doors for them. Because at a certain time, they also have other things to do. They can't keep receiving students looking for breakfast. So, around specials, I have my trash manager just dump whatever's there and hasn't been touched yet. . . . You know that nobody wants it, nobody needs it or whatever. The kids, they save the food for whoever comes in late. And some of them, like they'll like keep the fruit and take it home. . . . So that's what that system does, so everyone gets a chance or at least an opportunity to get it. And if I know a student needs it, I'll give them a moment, even it if means that like during warm-up, I may have them sit in the back of the classroom, go ahead and eat that and try to do your warm-up at the same time."

In setting up the food system in her classroom, Ms. Robinson was drawing on a rich tradition of self-help and mutual aid that has existed in historically marginalized communities in the United States and throughout the African diaspora.[6] Women from historically marginalized communities have played an essential and often overlooked role in creating feeding programs, health-care systems, and alternative banking systems as forms of resistance to racism and other forms of exclusion.[7] In Ms. Robinson's classroom, her efforts to create an inclusive and accessible feeding system was also helping to reproduce this tradition, as students actively participated in caring for each other as they offered unused breakfast items that could be used by their classmates who needed additional food.

At City Charter, teachers also provided food for students, most frequently during the school's morning snack time. Due to its extended day schedule, the school provided a morning snack time for students to sustain their energy between breakfast and a later lunch. While the school provided a time in the formal schedule for students to consume a snack, the school did not provide food for students to eat. Students were permitted to bring a snack from home or could eat the classroom snack; however, only a few students regularly brought snack from home.

To fill this gap, teachers relied on a combination of donations from family members who were able to afford to purchase food for the classroom and their own contributions to provide food for students to eat. Two teachers kept sign-up sheets on their classroom doors for parents to volunteer to provide the food students would consume during snack time. Another teacher assigned a different student to bring in snacks each week by posting the student's name next to "snack" or "snack next week" on the classroom whiteboard. "Some people don't sign up for snack, and I never really push them. I don't want them to have to tell me 'Oh, we can't,'" a teacher explained. When donations from families fell short, several teachers reported that they often purchased snacks for their classrooms instead of reaching out to families.

Caring for Students When They Are Sick or Need to Sleep

On an April morning at City Charter, Ms. Kelly is sitting at the front of the carpet in her first grade classroom. She is dressed in gray jeans and a navy blue blouse with purple and white flowers on it. "Turn and share with your partner," she whispers to the students and then crouches on the carpet to listen to their conversation. "Back to me," Ms. Kelly says, returning to the front of the room. "The great thing about reading across genres is that we have so many series in our classroom," she says to the students in an excited tone, opening her arms wide.

After dismissing students to various areas of the classroom to do independent reading, Ms. Kelly meets with a group of students on the carpet before moving back to the c-shaped table at the back of her classroom. Tanya, a student whom I perceive to be Black and female, her dark hair twisted into two pigtails, walks up to Ms. Kelly. Ms. Kelly places her palm on Tanya's forehead and then puts her palm on her forehead as if she is measuring Tanya's temperature. "Are you just tired?" Ms. Kelly asks Tanya. "Have your book so you can read while you are resting."

Tanya curls up with a book in a beanbag chair in the classroom library. Later, during snack time, Ms. Kelly asks another student to bring Tanya some graham crackers. Tanya sleeps through the morning snack time and morning meeting and is still sleeping while the other students leave for a music class. "That's a lesson I learned pretty early in my teaching career. If they are tired, let them sleep. They're not going to do anything anyway," Ms. Kelly explained to me during her planning break. "But always tell their parents. 'She slept for an hour and a half today,'" she adds, looking at the clock.

Ms. Kelly moves around the classroom, setting up several laptop computers for students to use during the class's guided reading time. "Tanya, are you waking up? You're waking up a little bit. Do you want to go to the bathroom and then get some snack? Did you have a good sleep? It looks like it was comfortable," she says. Tanya is sitting up and rubbing her eyes. Ms. Kelly turns to me. "Also, always ask them if they need to go to the bathroom," she says. Ms. Kelly turns her attention back to Tanya. "Thank you for telling me that you needed a nap," she says. Tanya walks to the front of the room, takes the bathroom pass, and then leaves the classroom.

Later that afternoon, Ms. Kelly sits at a table with Tanya and a second girl. Ms. Kelly hands books to the girls, and they start to read aloud as their teacher listens. One of the girls makes a buzzing sound as she reads a book about bees. Ms. Kelly listens quietly and writes notes in a binder as the girls read. "Do you know what narrow means?" Ms. Kelly asks Tanya after she reads the word. Tanya shakes her head no. "It means really thin," Ms. Kelly says, showing Tanya by holding her palms close to each other.

At City Charter, sometimes tending to students who were ill or sleepy meant meeting students' needs within the classroom, as Ms. Kelly did when Tanya appeared to be unwell. In this case, Ms. Kelly encouraged Tanya to rest and had a place in her classroom (the library) where Tanya could curl up on a beanbag chair and rest until she was ready to reengage in classroom activities. At other times, tending to the needs of a tired or ill student involved referring students to other school resources, including the school nurse.

In Ms. Washington's third grade classroom, Gabby, a student whom I perceived to be Latina and female, is resting with her head down on the c-shaped table at the back of the classroom with her pink fleece jacket covering her head.

The rest of the students are on the carpet discussing the strategies they used on the required end-of-year standardized test they recently completed. After the discussion, the students move to different areas of the room to start working on a writing assignment. Ms. Washington, who identifies as African American and female and is in her ninth year teaching at City Charter, walks over to where Gabby is resting and lifts the pink fleece off of her head. "You okay?" Ms. Washington asks her. Gabby doesn't move or respond. "It's Monday," Ms. Washington continues, as if responding for her and walks away from the table. A few moments later, Ms. Washington returns. She touches Gabby's head, and Gabby sits up. Ms. Washington tells Gabby to go see the nurse, and she leaves the classroom.

Teachers at City Charter were supported in their efforts to care for ill students by the presence of a full-time nurse that the school was able to access through the school district's partnership with a local hospital. This partnership meant that City Charter was one of the 50 percent of public schools in the United States whose students had access to a full-time school nurse.[8] At Oak Grove, budget cuts following the 2008 recession led to vacant school nurse positions going unfilled. As a result, the students at Oak Grove had intermittent access to a school nurse, who rotated among several schools.

On a cold, rainy morning in February, about a half dozen students are lined up next to Ms. Brown's desk, waiting to have their homework checked. Ms. Brown, who identifies as White and female, has been teaching at Oak Grove for the past thirteen years. Ms. Brown's first grade classroom is orderly and neat—the first thing she does at the end of a typical school day is to clean and straighten her room—and she expects the same from her students. Ms. Brown's emphasis on orderliness is also balanced with a sarcastic sense of humor that she deploys with students who she thinks can handle it. One of those students is Mateo, whom I perceive to be male and Latino. Mateo is wearing a gray zip-up sweater over his white uniform shirt and is standing next to Ms. Brown's desk with his homework.

"Did you eat breakfast at home?" Ms. Brown asks him, and Mateo shakes his head no. "You need to eat breakfast every day," Ms. Brown says to him. "Sit down for now. We'll see how you feel in a little bit."

About ten minutes later, Ms. Brown has begun a calendar math lesson with the students. She poses a question to the students and then calls on Mateo, who is now resting his head on his desk. "Sit up," Ms. Brown says to him. Mateo makes a pained expression and hugs his arms around his stomach. He sits up and answers the question Ms. Brown asks him correctly. Mateo remains sitting up for a minute or two and then leans over his desk, resting his head on one of his arms.

After calendar math, the students engage in a language lesson where they are asked to find "tricky words" on the smart board at the front of the class.

"Let's try this one," Ms. Brown says. She touches the screen, and a sentence appears. It says: "Did you have funn this weekend?" Several students offer suggestions for editing the sentence, including a student with thick-rimmed glasses who walks to the front of the room and corrects the spelling of "fun."

"Speaking of spelling, let's make our words. Get out your scissors," Ms. Brown directs the class. She drops a few strips of paper on each cluster of desks. "Snip your letters," Ms. Brown encourages the class. "Are we going to make any trash?" "No!" the students say in unison. "Snip your letters and put your scissors away," Ms. Brown instructs. The students cut the strips of paper Ms. Brown gave them into smaller squares. "Snip, snip, snip!" she cues the students.

Mateo burps. "Excuse you," Ms. Brown says and then seeing the queasy look on his face says, "Why don't you go to the nurse? I don't know if there is one, so good luck." Mateo walks quickly to the door and leaves.

About an hour later, Mateo returns from the school nurse while the other students are at music class. He says he does not have his mother's phone number to call her to take him home, and it does not appear as if the school or Ms. Brown have access to Mateo's mother's number either. Ms. Brown decides to keep Mateo in the classroom for the remainder of the day. For two hours, Mateo is able to participate in math and writing activities but starts to feel poorly again. Ms. Brown tells him to rest with his head down on his desk, and Mateo remains that way for most of the remaining two hours of the school day while the other students participate in reading activities and a practice standardized math test.

Developing Relationships with Students

In addition to responding to students' needs for food and a place to rest, teachers at Oak Grove and City Charter also sought to foster students' belonging and connection to school by developing relationships with students. Teachers did this in different ways. Some greeted students by name when they entered the classroom each morning; many shared details of their personal lives with students as part of introducing themselves at the beginning of the year or making connections to a lesson. Many teachers also created opportunities for students to share information about themselves as part of personalizing academic lessons or as a dedicated part of the school day.

In Ms. Jackson's third grade classroom, the students have just returned from their music class and are taking their seats at desks that are arranged in a horseshoe formation: two long lines of desks face each other at the sides of the classroom and a long line of desks facing the large blackboard at the front of the room connects them. Inside the horseshoe, smaller rows of desks face the blackboard. The structure of the physical space in Ms. Jackson's room mirrors her teaching style, which emphasizes opportunities for students to express themselves through activities like classroom-wide debates and small group projects. Ms. Jackson, who identifies as Black and female, is in her fourth year of teaching and first year of teaching at Oak Grove Elementary. After receiving her Bachelors in Elementary Education, Ms. Jackson taught for three years at a private Christian school in the same county before making the transition to Oak Grove.

Ms. Jackson is standing at the front of the classroom, next to an overhead projector. She is wearing a long white cable knit sweater over fitted navy blue pants. Her hair is straightened and falls a few inches below her shoulders. "Alright, number of the day," Ms. Jackson says projecting the small whiteboard on the screen pulled down over the blackboard.

Several students in the class are talking about pictures that they want Ms. Jackson to show them. "I showed them to you at the beginning of the year," Ms. Jackson says, laughing, seeming surprised that the students are so interested in seeing them again. Eventually, she pauses the math lesson to project what looks like a PowerPoint slide. The background is yellow, and there is bulleted text above three pictures. The text says:

WHY AM I A TEACHER?
- I love making an impact on students.
- I love being creative and energetic.
- Not only can you learn from me but I can learn from you!

The pictures below the text look like they are of Ms. Jackson with students at her former school. Ms. Jackson moves on to the next slide which includes a picture of Ms. Jackson in a graduation cap and gown next to a logo from her alma mater, a public state university.

At her students' encouragement, Ms. Jackson was revisiting a presentation that she had given at the beginning of the school year when she was introducing herself to her students. She had shared information about her previous job, her college degree, and also about her philosophy of education—that it was a two-way process. As will be discussed more in Chapter 2, Ms. Jackson provided many opportunities for students to share information about their lives and make personal connections to the curriculum, two elements of culturally responsive education.[9] This instance demonstrated that Ms. Jackson was willing to do the same—to share information about her personal life and her personal connections to education.

Ms. Jackson's third grade team member, Ms. Robinson, also took advantage of opportunities to connect with students around their lives outside school. Ms. Robinson frequently built in opportunities for students to personalize their academic assignments and offered information about her family or her experience immigrating to the United States as examples and points of connection with students.

In Ms. Robinson's classroom, the students are gathered on the carpet at the front of the room, with some spilling over into the chairs at the edges of the carpet. "Boys and girls, yesterday—I'll wait—yesterday, we talked about things you are passionate about. I want you to high five a partner and tell them something you are passionate about," Ms. Robinson says. The students begin to talk to each other. A few moments later, Ms. Robinson rings a bell. "3, 2, 1," she says slowly. "Okay. So, now, I am going to choose three people to share what they are passionate about." Students begin to share: "Drawing." "My game: Call of Duty Ghosts."

"I am passionate about Honduras," a student who I perceived to be female says. "She is passionate about her country. That is awesome because Ms. Robinson is passionate about her country, too," Ms. Robinson says after students seem to be confused about their peer's response.

Helping Students Relate to Each Other

On a warm spring morning in May, the students in Ms. Washington's third grade classroom are sitting on the carpet with their assistant teacher Ms. Lowery. Ms. Lowery, who identifies as Black and female, is in her third year of working at City Charter. Today, she is leading the classroom's morning meeting. "So, we're going to do a turn and talk about Mother's Day or what happened this weekend. When I say one, turn to your partner but don't talk. I want to see where our partners are. One. Okay," Ms. Lowery instructs and then pauses. She pairs up a few students who are missing partners. "On two, I want you to share about your weekend including if you celebrated Mother's Day. Two," Ms. Lowery says. The students begin talking to each other. "Okay, turn back in 3, 2, 1. Thank you. Good job," Ms. Lowery praises the students.

In many classrooms at City Charter and Oak Grove, teachers provide structured opportunities for students to communicate and build relationships with their peers. In City Charter, these opportunities were often included as part of the school's practice of holding morning meetings, where students had opportunities to share information about what was happening in their lives outside school. At Oak Grove Elementary, these opportunities were often integrated with academic learning, as Ms. Robinson did when she had students discuss what they were passionate about as a topic for a writing assignment.

Connecting with Students' Families

One morning in Ms. Robinson's third grade classroom, she was using some of her planning time to meet with one of her students, Micah, while the rest of the students were at music class. Micah was absent from class yesterday, and Ms. Robinson tells him that she is going to call his father so that she can set up a time to meet with him for a conference. Micah says that he doesn't know his father's phone number. "That's your responsibility to know," Ms. Robinson replies in a calm, even tone. Ms. Robinson tells Micah that she has had difficulty contacting his father and mother because their phone numbers are disconnected and asks him how he gets home after school. Micah says that sometimes his mother picks him up and sometimes his father picks him up. Ms. Robinson says that she will wait with him or walk home with him so that she can set up a time for a parent conference.

Ms. Robinson tells Micah that she thinks he can do better in terms of his behavior and grades and that she wants to see him do better. "What do you think you can do to improve?" she asks him. Micah says that he can stop talking to other students, something that Ms. Robinson warned him about while the students were taking a standardized reading test earlier today. Ms. Robinson dismisses Micah. After he leaves the classroom, Ms. Robinson says that she is frustrated because Micah is so lazy. "He is capable. He just doesn't want to do the work," she says. She adds that she has had difficulty contacting his parents but that she feels that she really needs to speak with them at this point. "So, I'll put on my hat and my scarf," she says, referring to the chilly December weather that day.

About a month and a half later, I ask Ms. Robinson how the visit went. Ms. Robinson said that she walked with Micah to one of the apartment complexes that surround the school where he waits for his mother to pick him up. After about four or five minutes of waiting, Micah saw his stepmother walking toward him, and Ms. Robinson asked her if she could talk with her. Ms. Robinson recalled that she was concerned about Micah's motivation and that after the conversation, she realized that this may be related to the fact that he is not getting enough sleep at night. Ms. Robinson learned that Micah's father works a late shift and usually arrives home at 11:00 P.M. for dinner. In order to spend time with his dad, Micah often comes home from school, takes a nap, wakes up to eat dinner with his family around 11:00 P.M., and then returns to bed around 1:00 A.M. Given that school starts at 7:30 A.M. the next morning, Ms. Robinson realized that Micah is likely only getting five to six hours of continuous sleep per night.

Taking the time to meet with Micah's stepmother after school allowed Ms. Robinson to better understand the challenge that Micah and his family were facing as they tried to negotiate a way to have a family dinner together around the boundaries of Micah's father's workday. The additional work that Ms. Robinson did to reach out to Micah's family allowed her to revise her initial perception of Micah as a "lazy" student and to see how the structure of Micah's father's employment was influencing how and when Micah was able to sleep. Ms. Robinson shared that she felt positively about the interaction because she was able to obtain working phone numbers for Micah's family members. This would allow her to continue to touch base with Micah's family and to keep the lines of communication open.

While this example was the only instance I encountered of a teacher conducting a home visit, teachers at both Oak Grove and City Charter regularly communicated with and sought to foster connections with students' families. Methods of connecting to students' family members included informal conversations as parents dropped off or picked up their students at the beginning and end of the school day. They also included teachers calling home to share with parents a success or challenge that their child had experienced during the school day. Some teachers also communicated with parents by text or handwritten notes.

As these examples demonstrate, teachers' work at Oak Grove Elementary and City Charter included not only the work of teaching students academic content but labor that was oriented to making sure that students could take full advantage of academic learning. This work involved providing food for students, caring for students when they were ill or tired, helping students create connections to their teacher and their peers, and building and maintaining relationships with students' family members. In the chapters that follow, I turn to the factors that shaped teachers' work as they sought to meet students' social, emotional, and material needs and show how teachers' work is constrained and enabled by school reform policies, the resources that are available at their school, and the presence or absence of school-wide practices, such as social and emotional learning curricula.

Part 2
Oak Grove Elementary
• •

2

Working in an
Audit Culture

● ●

Surveillance and Teaching at
Oak Grove Elementary

On a February afternoon at Oak Grove Elementary, Ms. Phillips and I are seated at a small c-shaped table in the front corner of her classroom. It is 2:10 P.M. and Ms. Phillips has already dismissed her students for the day, a procedure that was made more difficult than usual due to the several inches of snow that are blanketing the sidewalks outside the school. Oak Grove Elementary School is a traditional public school located in a suburb of a city in the mid-Atlantic region of the United States. The school was built in the 1960s as part of a community of garden-style apartments that were established at a time when increased transportation and real estate development, together with successful social movements for fair housing practices, led to the desegregation of the larger Oak Grove community. Oak Grove Elementary continues to draw most of its students from the surrounding neighborhood. During the school year that I observed at Oak Grove (2013–2014), 85 percent of students were eligible for free and reduced-price school meals. More than half the students identified as Hispanic/Latino and over 40 percent identified as Black/African American.

Ms. Phillips, a second grade teacher who identifies as White and female, is about halfway through her fifteenth year teaching at Oak Grove. On this February afternoon, we are talking about some of the more challenging aspects of her job, including the school's new teacher evaluation system.

"Honestly, I think it's the paperwork that's coming down the pike," Ms. Phillips says when I ask her about the most challenging part of her job. "It's so much data-keeping. . . . I see the value of data but so much of it is just useless. It doesn't help me. So, if it's not helping me, I don't know who else would want it. . . . And it seems like we've been getting more and more and more of that stuff. I don't see the value of it, so I'm not interested in doing it. And probably don't do the best job at it."

The additional paperwork that Ms. Phillips is referring to is part of the school's new teacher evaluation system that the school district created as part of its Race to the Top federal grant application. Created in 2008, Race to the Top was a competitive grant program that incentivized school districts to use student assessment data as part of their teacher evaluation systems. The program provided $4.35 billion to states that committed to use "student growth" data—defined as standardized testing scores for tested subjects and alternative assessments for non-tested subjects—in their evaluations of teachers' and administrators' work.[1] A highly effective teacher, as defined by the Race to the Top grant solicitation, is one "whose students achieve high rates (e.g., one and one-half grade levels in an academic year) of student growth."[2]

The new teacher evaluation system at Oak Grove Elementary had several different components. One component required teachers to select their own set of learning objectives (based on state standards) to use to track a subset of their students' progress. Teachers were required to create a goal related to the number of students who would meet these objectives and to track the selected students' progress in meeting the learning objectives. While this provision offered some flexibility to teachers, it seemed confusing and duplicative to Ms. Phillips who wondered why additional data collection and reporting was required in addition to what her school and school district already required. "I don't mind keeping data . . . like I love to look at my DRA [Diagnostic Reading Assessment] data. I love looking, okay, this is where they were in August, and then in October and December. It's like yay! I really like that . . . I don't mind keeping data that is useful to me, and I do it on my own," she says.

Ms. Phillips also worried that another component of the evaluation system, the use of standardized assessments that required teachers to report only whether a child was performing above or below grade level, didn't allow for any recognition of the ongoing progress that she saw her students making. She gives an example of what she observed with one of her students, Eli.

"For somebody like Eli, I did a sight word checklist with him, and he did phenomenally. His reading level has gone up a lot since the beginning of the school year. And we did another checklist last week, and it was just so exciting to see he's actually not just reading [and] barely spitting out [the words] . . . he was reading the story, and he was laughing as he was reading it, which means he got the joke of it and the fun of it, so he really was understanding a book," she explained. "To me, that was really encouraging to see him reading and truly understanding it, enjoying the book! It's like, you're a reader. You did it. You crossed that line."

Ms. Phillips' experiences teaching reading and her interactions with Eli suggested to her that he had made an important transition from being able to read and pronounce words to being able to comprehend and find enjoyment in reading a portion of a book. However, Eli was still considered to be below grade level by the standardized assessment that Ms. Phillips used to track her students' reading progress. "I try to explain . . . there's a huge jump from reading [the beginner books] to reading something that they can laugh at and get it. That is such an improvement but somehow [my administrator] doesn't see that because it's still far below grade level. It is, but it's been a tremendous amount of progress," Ms. Phillips says.

The disconnect Ms. Phillips is describing between her observations of a student's progress and what type of progress counts for her formal teaching observation was characteristic of the ways that school reform policies shaped teachers' work at Oak Grove Elementary. In the audit culture of school reform policies, students' and teachers' progress was standardized and measured in ways that did not reflect individual students' assets and progress and individual teachers' local context, knowledge, and expertise. Moreover, the audit culture of school reform policies contributed to a multilevel system of surveillance that classified and graded schools based on their achievement outputs, reduced the autonomy that teachers had to control their work and interact in particular ways with students, and limited students' abilities to engage in meaningful learning experiences. This chapter examines the audit culture of school reform policies and their relationship to teachers' work at Oak Grove Elementary. It explores the ways that an audit culture constrains teachers' work and the ways that teachers resist constraints on their autonomy.

Teaching in an Audit Culture

Accountability policies, such as the No Child Left Behind Act of 2001 (NCLB) and Race to the Top, have been characterized as examples of an audit culture, "contexts in which the techniques and values of accountancy have become a central organizing principle in the governance and management of human conduct."[3] Audits, which originally were used to regulate financial institutions, have been expanded to the spheres of government, health care, education, and environmental policy.[4] Audits rely on the knowledge of "experts" to assess the efficiency, value, and performance of a particular institution or program. Audit knowledge is built and legitimized through the credibility of experts, abstract quality control systems, and detailed practices of measurement.[5]

An audit culture reflects the ways in which the principles of accountancy come to shape the lived experiences of individuals. As Cris Shore explains:

> audit changes the way people perceive themselves: it encourages them to measure themselves and their personal qualities against the external "benchmarks", "performance indicators" and "ratings" used by the auditing process. An audit society is one where people are interpolated as auditees, where accountability is conflated with elaborate policing mechanisms for subjecting individual performance to the gaze of external experts, and where every aspect of work must be ranked and assessed against bureaucratic benchmarks and economic targets.[6]

The proliferation of audit cultures has led to the recentralization and de-democratization of institutions and extended mechanisms of surveillance to teachers' work and students' learning, where they intersected with existing gendered and racialized social processes.[7] At Oak Grove, I observed many examples of administrators' and teachers' autonomy and voice being supplanted by school reform requirements, including as part of the district's extensive teacher evaluation system. Requiring teachers to closely document their work while reducing the control they had over it intersects with a history of associating teaching with "women's work" and of devaluing this work when assigning compensation and professional status.[8] Standardized testing policies also played a role in structuring students' learning opportunities, from the amount of time that students were required to engage in testing to the limits that were placed on students' abilities to interact and move their bodies during testing periods, a theme that is discussed in more detail in Chapter 3. These forms of control intersected with the many forms of racialized social control that research has demonstrated that students experience inside and outside schools, including school discipline policies and police surveillance.[9] As this chapter demonstrates, the audit culture of accountability placed constraints on teachers' work that made it more difficult for them to achieve the stated aims of school reform policies and their own internalized notions of what it meant to be a good teacher.

Surveillance and Accountability at Oak Grove Elementary

As a traditional public school that was labeled as "needing improvement" by the requirements of NCLB, Oak Grove Elementary was under regular surveillance. This surveillance took the form of frequent observations from administrators and multiple levels of school district staff. Surveillance also occurred through the production, documentation, and at times publication of numerous forms of evidence related to teaching and learning.

During my first observation at Oak Grove, I visited the classroom of Ms. Lewis, a first-year teacher who identified as White and female. Ms. Lewis shared her trepidation about feeling unprepared on the same day that the school was being observed by representatives from the school district's regional office. She had received an email that morning from her principal notifying teachers that members of the school district's regional office would be visiting the school that day to conduct observations. These observations were taking place a week before representatives from the superintendent's office would be conducting their own round of observations.

Ms. Lewis's fear about the consequences of appearing unprepared were mirrored one morning about a month later when an administrator reminded teachers and students at the end of morning announcements that "we are having visitors today, so we appreciate everyone [the administrator pauses as if choosing her words carefully] showing their best." At Oak Grove Elementary, teachers were subject to announced and unannounced observations from their administrators, regional office staff, and school district staff. School administrators and teachers were expected to accommodate requests for observations and other forms of data collection and to adjust their instructional plans and activities with students to align with these requirements.

In addition to frequent visits from school officials, surveillance of teachers at Oak Grove Elementary also took the form of the significant amounts of data the school and its teachers were asked to produce to demonstrate their students' progress. Each year, the school was required to administer a series of standardized assessments to meet the requirements of NCLB. Oak Grove Elementary was also required by its school district to administer a standardized reading comprehension test four times a year to determine whether students were reading above grade level, on grade level, or below grade level. Students in the school's English for Speakers of Other Languages (ESOL) program—about 40 percent of students at Oak Grove—were required to take a separate assessment during the winter months to assess their progress in the program. These assessments were in addition to the assessments that teachers implemented at the classroom level to track their students' progress in mastering curriculum standards, including math tests, spelling tests, science and social studies tests, writing assessments, and the Diagnostic Reading Assessment described earlier by Ms. Phillips.

While some of these assessments were lower stakes and diagnostic—allowing teachers to track their students' progress and adjust instruction accordingly—others came with significant consequences if the school could not demonstrate that it had improved student achievement. NCLB created a system of accountability for public schools in which all schools receiving federal education funding are required to test students in particular grades in reading, math, and science each year and to report students' progress in meeting achievement targets. Title I schools—schools that serve high numbers or high percentages of students from economically disadvantaged families, such as Oak Grove Elementary—are subject to additional requirements. Due to the intersection of racial and economic inequities, this means that schools that serve a high percentage of students of color are also often subjected to these requirements. Under NCLB, Title I schools are required to meet annual testing targets set by their state (defined as "adequate yearly progress"), and those that continuously fail to meet these targets face a series of progressive sanctions. Schools that consistently fail to demonstrate that they can improve their students' test scores can be subject to closure, and teachers working at these schools can be required to reapply for their positions in the newly reconstituted school.

In 2002, the year that NCLB was signed into law, 58 percent of all public schools (47,600) were classified as Title I schools and subject to the "adequate yearly progress" provisions of NCLB.[10] Five years later, about 4,500 Title I schools had failed to meet their standardized testing targets for four or more years and 2,790 of these schools had been selected for corrective action or restructuring, meaning that they had been required to make a significant change in how their school is organized, including changes to the school's curriculum, administration, and teaching staff.[11]

In Oak Grove Elementary's school district, the threat of sanctions for schools that failed to meet standardized testing expectations was real. In 2009—three years before I observed at Oak Grove Elementary—the middle school that serves Oak Grove Elementary's students had undergone a process of "alternative governance," in which its administrators and several teachers were replaced after the school had failed to meet standardized testing targets for reading and math. During the year I observed at Oak Grove Elementary, the school had been classified in the second to last tier of schools in its state because it had not met any of its achievement targets that year, according to data published on the state education agency's website.

Policy vs. Practice: Teacher Evaluation at Oak Grove Elementary

In 2013, Scholastic and the Bill & Melinda Gates Foundation surveyed more than 20,000 public school teachers about their experiences working in schools and classrooms, including the extent to which their opinions are heard and valued within their schools and the larger policy context. The majority of teachers surveyed reported that they were heard and valued within their school. However, slightly less than a third said that their opinions were valued when decisions are made by school district officials at least most of the time and even fewer when decisions are made at the state and federal level.[12] This disconnect between education reform policymaking and teachers' experience was reflected at Oak Grove Elementary, including in the implementation of the school district's new teacher evaluation system. Teachers at Oak Grove regularly engaged in their own forms of assessment and self-evaluation but, unlike those required by school reform policies, these tended to be informal and integrated into the daily rhythm of their teaching work.

Ms. Brown, a first grade teacher at Oak Grove Elementary who has been teaching for sixteen years, describes the work she does each day after school. "The first thing I do is clean up from the day and just get today out of the way. And then I start looking at what I have for tomorrow. Do I need to change what I'm teaching tomorrow, like did today's math lesson go terribly and whoops, I can't do what I planned for the next day, so I need to reteach it? So, I don't necessarily grade the papers from the day, but I might glance through them if I need. But I also think about how did that math lesson go? Did I see them really struggling or can I go on to this in reading? Or did we get really stuck in this one conversation in reading, and I can't go to the next part?"

The evaluation and self-reflection that Ms. Brown engaged in as a matter of course at the end of each day had recently been formalized as an additional component of the teacher evaluation system at Oak Grove Elementary. As part of the new evaluation system, teachers at Oak Grove were required to complete a lengthy self-assessment form—one teacher's form was twelve single-spaced typed pages—detailing a single lesson plan that would be reviewed by a school administrator. After reviewing the document, the administrator provided feedback to the teacher, who was then required to revise the lesson plan to incorporate this feedback. Once sufficient revisions had been made, the teacher was then required to deliver the lesson and was evaluated based on an administrator's observation of the lesson. The administrator was then expected to type up a set of formal notes based on the observation, to rate the teacher's performance on a standardized scale, and to schedule a conference with the teacher to discuss the results. At the end of the conference, the teacher was required to sign the evaluation document, acknowledging that the discussion had occurred.

The procedures for this evaluation closely tracked the informal self-assessment that Ms. Brown described engaging in at the end of the school day. However, while Ms. Brown completed this process as a matter of course each day, the formalized version of this process took a significant amount of time and resources at the school. Teachers who were tenured were required to undergo the formalized evaluation process twice a year; newer, untenured teachers were required to engage in the process four times a year. This meant that the school's principal and assistant principal were required to conduct multiple observations for all forty-six teachers at the school. Depending on the balance of tenured and untenured teachers in a given year, administrators were required to complete between 92 and 184 evaluation observations and conferences within that year. Given that the school year at Oak Grove Elementary was set by the state at a required 180 days, an administrator would have to complete a formal classroom observation at least once every other day. (In the year that I observed, the administrators had the aid of an administrator-in-training who helped to complete some elements of the teacher observation process.) This lengthy and time-consuming process was one example in which the audit culture of school reform policies transformed an informal and taken-for-granted aspect teachers' work—critical reflection—into a highly routinized form of surveillance. It also diverted teachers' and administrators' time and attention from meeting students' needs to the production of extensive documentation and proof that these needs were being met.

Ms. Jackson, a third grade teacher at Oak Grove Elementary compared the highly formalized ritual of her current teacher evaluation process to what she had experienced teaching at a private school. "This one [the teacher evaluation system at Oak Grove Elementary] is actually like kinda intense from what I saw. Here, we have four formal observations if you're not tenured. So, I have to do four formal for the next three years until I'm tenured, so I have one like every single quarter, a formal observation. That's only one part of my evaluation. Then, I have their test scores. Then, we have student learning objectives, so I pick a group and it's based on their growth academically, so I'm evaluated on that, like if I've met my target or not on their growth. And they took student surveys, so how do the students feel about me. That's part of the evaluation, and I think there's one more part, I don't remember. So, it's kind of intense these evaluations. At my old school, it wasn't that intense. Like, they come in a couple times. But we met every single week, so I kinda knew what I needed maybe to do better on, so it wasn't as intense as it is here. It's really intense. And our evaluations [at the private school] weren't based on test scores or student surveys, any of that. It was based on just me as a teacher and my delivery of lessons, that's what it was. That's way different. Totally different."

The lengthy teacher evaluation process appeared to place burdens on both teachers and administrators, reflected in Ms. Jackson's characterization of the evaluation system as "intense." The intensity of the evaluation system was reflected in the amount of time teachers and administrators spent engaging in required evaluation activities and producing the paperwork documenting that evaluation activities had been completed. An administrator-in-training at the school described a typical day as "hectic." "This morning I did two formal observations, two post-observations, three informal observations, typically 15 to 20 minutes in three different classrooms. In two teachers' classrooms, questions came up—I just did an intervention with two teachers about transitions [students moving from one activity to another] that were taking too long. In fifteen minutes, I have a School Planning Management Team meeting. One of the teachers got an award from Oak Grove ACE, which is kind of like the

Rotary Club or City Council . . . so I'm going out at 8 P.M. this evening [to see her receive the award]."

The intensity of the evaluation system was also reflected in its relationship to teachers' future employment and pay. While the evaluation system was only in the pilot stage during the year that I observed at Oak Grove Elementary, the following year teachers would be evaluated, in part, based on their students' test scores. Several teachers expressed worry about whether the new evaluation system would accurately reflect their performance as a teacher and whether the school district officials designing the evaluation would take contextual factors into account, such as the challenges their students faced at home or the difficulty of motivating students to take standardized tests seriously.

The high-stakes nature of the teacher evaluation system combined with the alienation teachers felt from decision-making processes at district and federal levels created a challenging situation for teachers at Oak Grove Elementary, where they understood the importance of complying with evaluation activities but saw little intrinsic value in this work. Teachers described evaluation activities as "checking the box"—doing what they needed to do to fulfill a requirement that was imposed externally. Ms. Robinson described a type of resigned optimism that she took to completing the evaluation requirements. "I was like okay, let me just turn that in and just continue teaching because I know at the end [of the school year], they [the students] will do better," she said. "This whole administrative process, it was like why? I'm still doing what I gotta do."

Ms. Robinson's statement underscores several key elements in the ways that teachers related to school reform policies at Oak Grove Elementary. Teachers often saw evaluation activities as separate from their teaching practice—"let me just turn that in and just continue teaching." And while teachers questioned aspects of the evaluation system to me or in conversations with each other, I did not see much evidence that these concerns were being raised to school district officials or that there were opportunities to do so. Only once did a teacher mention raising a concern at the district level, and this concern related to curriculum rather than school reform policies. This teacher was Ms. Brown who, in the midst of describing how she wished the school district would listen to more feedback from teachers, remembered an experience she'd had with the school district's math department. "I wish they took more feedback from us, which the math department did last year, that was good. I came back from math meeting very pleasantly surprised at the feedback they took, and we saw those changes," she said.

Ms. Brown's work on the school leadership team and as the school's first grade department chair, may have placed her in a more advantageous position to be able to communicate with school district officials. More common, however, in teachers' conversations with each other and with me, was the approach that Ms. Phillips had decided to take. "I feel like as a teacher you know you just do what you're told," Ms. Phillips said. "Why are we not doing that?" she asked, referring to a new assessment process at the school. "I don't know. But I just do as I'm told."

Constrained Collegiality

Teacher autonomy has been found to be an important predictor of teachers' job satisfaction and their willingness to remain in the profession.[13] When teachers have more control over their work and their work environment, they tend to stay in their local school and in the teaching profession longer. Evidence from the National Schools and Staffing Survey, which provides nationally representative estimates of teachers' working conditions, suggests that teachers' perceptions of their autonomy have declined in the decade after the implementation of NCLB.[14] During the 2003–2004 school year, 18 percent of teachers reported that they had little autonomy in their school, as measured by their perceived control over areas such as selecting textbooks and classroom materials and selecting content and skills to be taught. By the 2011–2012 school year, 26 percent of teachers reported low autonomy at their school.

Research examining the influence of school reform policies on teacher autonomy has also found that teachers' perceived control over key elements of their classroom policy can influence how they teach and interact with students.[15]

At Oak Grove Elementary, the audit-driven nature of school reform policies seemed to spill over into teachers' interactions with each other, particularly in formalized settings like regular department meetings. This was particularly notable in the first grade teachers' team meetings, which were often highly structured and designed to produce particular outcomes, with these outcomes documented by a designated note-taker.

On a Tuesday morning at Oak Grove Elementary, six first grade teachers are sitting at student desks in Ms. Brown's classroom. They have gathered for their regular Tuesday department meeting while their students are attending "specials" classes like physical education and music. That morning's announcements had included a reminder to teachers that they need to sign in if they attend a meeting in order to comply with an accountability requirement.

Ms. Brown, the first grade department chair, starts the meeting by stating the objective of the meeting—to review a dictation assignment the first grade students recently completed and to develop a ten-day plan for what the teachers need to work on with students based on their review of the assignment. A sign-in sheet is being passed around for teachers to indicate that they have attended the meeting, and Ms. Brown asks for a volunteer to take meeting notes. I am asked by two different people if I would like to sign the sign-in sheet, and I demur. (In subsequent meetings, I will be asked to sign the sign-in sheet to indicate my presence.)

Ms. Brown calls on Ms. Lewis to be the first teacher to share how her students performed on the dictation assignment. Ms. Lewis says that many of her students had difficulty writing the letter "m" and that many also had trouble spelling the word "park." Ms. Brown said that she saw similar trends among her students. Ms. Lewis says that students were only using the letters "p, r, and k" to spell the word. "If you think about it, those are the sounds that they hear," the teacher taking the notes says. There is some discussion about how the teachers scored the assignments. One teacher said she used "conventions of learning and sentences." "I scored in three parts," Ms. Brown said.

Ms. Brown calls on another first grade teacher, Ms. Callahan, next. Ms. Callahan flips through her students' papers, which are resting in a stack on the desk in front of her. "Do you have this?" Ms. Brown asks, holding up a worksheet. "No," Ms. Callahan says. "Can you tell me why?" Ms. Brown asks in a clipped tone. "It must have slipped my mind," Ms. Callahan says. "Okay," Ms. Brown says, looking displeased, and moves on to the next teacher. By now, two additional teachers have joined the group. "Room 15," Ms. Brown says, referring to those two teachers. The English for Speakers of other Languages (ESOL) teacher of the pair mentions a lack of punctuation as an area for improvement. Her co-teacher mentions that she saw a lot of students write "pork" instead of "park." "I got some pork, too," Ms. Brown says. "I didn't get any pork," the teacher taking notes says. It is a light moment in an otherwise fairly formal and structured conversation.

"So, what kind of strategies do we want to put into place?" Ms. Brown asks after each teacher has shared their classroom's results. "You're saying interactive and guided writing," Ms. Brown says, referring to the teacher who is taking notes. "I'm saying interactive writing, which I'm already doing but just more focused," she adds, speaking for herself.

"So, we're supposed to write a new standard?" Ms. Brown asks. There seems to be some confusion among the teachers about how to fill out the remainder of the worksheet that they are required to complete to document the meeting.

"So, standards for review, I guess we could put 1A and 1B," says the teacher taking notes.

"All of them? The standards aren't worded that way but we want students to be able to look at a sentence and correct it," Ms. Brown says as she tries to figure out how to align the skill that she has identified that her students need to work on with the wording in the school district's official standards.

"Is there a standard for editing?" Ms. Brown wonders aloud. "It says production and distribution but not editing." Ms. Brown consults a notebook with another teacher sitting near her. "Ah, found it," she says. "Demonstrate the standard of . . . It's L.1.2. I know you all just wrote that down."

From the sign-in sheet to Ms. Brown's pointed reminder to teachers—"I know you all just wrote that down"—the first grade team meeting reproduced many of the forms of hierarchy and control embedded in school reform policies, demonstrating that these extended to teachers' interactions at the school. The meeting had a clearly defined structure—with Ms. Brown taking the leadership role and calling on other teachers to report on their progress. The sign-in sheet and designation of a teacher to take notes ensured that the meeting would be documented for the school's administrator and any outside observers. The meeting also provided another instance of a clash between teachers' folk knowledge and the language of school reform policies, when teachers had a clear sense of how they would like to adjust their instruction but had to find the appropriate language in their state standards to communicate their plans. In this instance, the language of school reform policies presented a potential barrier to teachers being able to express and document their work. Different hierarchies of control and autonomy are also present in teachers' interactions—including the deference that (most of) the other teachers afforded Ms. Brown and the deference that the teachers made to the language of school reform policies.

While some teachers, such as Ms. Brown, could exercise a certain degree of autonomy and leadership within a particular context at Oak Grove Elementary, this autonomy appeared to be easily eclipsed when it became a matter of complying with a school reform requirement. The following week, the first grade teachers are once again gathered for their team meeting. The teachers are discussing their plans for the next reading unit when a woman comes into Ms. Brown's room and interrupts the discussion to ask Ms. Brown when would be a good time to come to her classroom to do a student survey today. Earlier that day, on the morning announcements, there had been a brief mention of the implementation of another component of the new teacher evaluation system: the survey of students and their perceptions of the classroom climate. "We are trying to complete the student surveys today," the morning announcer had said. "Teachers, thank you for your cooperation."

Ms. Brown turns toward the woman who has just entered her room to schedule the survey. "How long will it take?" Ms. Brown asks her. "About an hour," she responds without apology or irony. Ms. Brown's expression shifts to one of utter disbelief, possibly with some dismay mixed in. "I don't have an hour block," she says.

"I don't have an hour block in my day," she says again and begins to describe her daily schedule to the woman to demonstrate that she does not, in fact, have a single uninterrupted hour of instructional time. Ms. Brown gets to the afternoon portion of her schedule, where she is with her students for a longer block of time, and then says "that's my groups," with some frustration, referring to the time when she meets with students in small groups for reading instruction.

"How many questions is it?" Ms. Brown asks the woman, referring to the survey. "Nineteen," the woman says. "And that takes an hour?" Ms. Brown asks incredulously. Ms. Callahan confirms that it did for her class and that her students missed participating in their specials class due to the survey. Ms. Brown and the woman administering the survey agree that she can come back during the time between specials classes. "That will work," Ms. Brown says, seeming somewhat relieved.

While Ms. Brown clearly occupied a leadership role during her team meetings, this power dynamic shifted quickly when the external demands of school reform policies were in play. The language of the morning announcement— "We are trying to complete the student surveys today. Teachers, thank you for your cooperation."—left little room for teachers' (or likely administrators') feedback or negotiation on the matter. In this case, Ms. Brown was able to negotiate with the school official to choose a time for the survey—a privilege that was not afforded a first-year teacher later that day—but she also was required to give up an hour of her instructional time on a particular day with very little notice.

How Teachers Define Good Teaching

The "high-stakes" nature of the teacher evaluation system combined with the alienation teachers felt from decision-making processes related to standardized testing and curricula created a challenging situation for teachers at Oak Grove Elementary. Teachers understood the importance of complying with evaluation activities but saw little intrinsic value in this work. Teachers described evaluation activities as "checking the box"—doing what they needed to do to fulfill a requirement that was imposed externally.

While many teachers felt alienated from standardized forms of assessment, in interviews several teachers at Oak Grove Elementary described their own internalized notions of what it meant to be an effective teacher. Teachers' definitions of effective teaching were generally directed toward the responsibility they felt for their students rather than toward an audience external to their classroom. Teachers' notions of what it meant to be a good teacher often involved the work of differentiating academic lessons to meet individual students' needs. It also frequently included engagement, relational work, and the academic outcomes that could flow from connections between students and teachers, between students and an assignment they were working on, or between students and their peers.

During an interview one afternoon in March, I ask Ms. Brown if she is planning to come back to teach at Oak Grove next year. "I definitely want to be, I used to say I will be in the classroom forever. Only recently have I thought because of just, to be honest some health issues I have, I can't always put in the hours that I require of myself as a teacher," Ms. Brown explains. "And I don't see a way to modify my teaching. Especially since things are changing, I can't just pull out my file and copy these papers and plan this. It's not like that any—I was never like that—I'm not that kind of teacher. Like the way, even before Common Core, I taught addition. This year, I know my kids need to do this but they're not going to be able to do it that way, so we're going to do it this way. I sat down and analyzed every single lesson. Math, reading, whatever. It's different every year. The kids are different, so I can pull out my file on life cycles but I might need to tweak it for this group. Maybe they have this much more background knowledge . . . I tweak it every year because every group is different."

Ms. Brown discusses her internalized notion of a "good teacher"—one that is willing to spend time learning about her students' existing knowledge and tailoring lessons to meet their needs. She differentiates herself from teachers who would simply repeat the same lessons year after year. This type of labor took a significant amount of time outside of the school day. When I asked Ms. Brown to describe a typical day working at Oak Grove Elementary, she described arriving at school around 6:30 A.M.—forty-five minutes before teachers were contractually required to arrive—to prepare her room for the day. After school, she will typically stay an additional hour or two to review students' assignments and revise plans and prepare materials for the next day. One exception is Thursday nights, which are Ms. Brown's late nights. "Later than late," she says. "I've been here until 8 or 9:00 sometimes, because I try to at least map out 'I'm doing this lesson and this lesson and this lesson' and get materials ready for that lesson but then I'll sit down later and be more specific about the parts of it."

Ms. Brown estimates that she works, on average, about ten hours per day during the work week and about sixty-five hours per week, including time spent working on the weekends. This time includes the work that Ms. Brown does for four paid jobs at Oak Grove Elementary: classroom teacher, department chair, school leadership team facilitator, and reading club organizer. The number of hours that Ms. Brown reported working is similar to the number of hours that teachers nationwide report spending on teaching-related activities. In a 2012 survey of more than 10,000 teachers in the United States, teachers said that, on average, they spend close to eleven hours working each day, including their required contract hours, time spent at school before and after school hours, and time spent working on teaching-related activities at home.[16]

Working beyond contractual hours, as Ms. Brown and many other teachers do, is a form of overwork. While union contracts guarantee that teachers cannot be required to work above a certain number of hours, in reality schools rely on the unpaid labor of teachers to function. As Lora Bartlett notes, "In fact, teachers dramatically slow and disrupt the work of a school when labour actions result in work that is in strict compliance with the terms of the contract, or simply 'working to rule.'"[17] School reform policies and efforts to gain professional recognition for the work of teaching have expanded teachers' scope of work to include developing curricula and assessment systems and tracking students' progress across classrooms. The expansion of teachers' roles has both advantages and disadvantages, as Bartlett describes, "Teachers who embrace the expanded role may experience greater satisfaction and commitment to the profession, but they may also experience a work overload that exhausts their enthusiasm and erodes their commitment."[18] At Oak Grove Elementary, school reform policy requirements such as the teacher evaluation system and standardized testing appeared to add to teachers' workload while also decreasing their autonomy and control over their work. These requirements also diverted teachers' time and attention away from the aspects of their work that they valued the most and that they saw as critical to student learning.

A "Good Day" at Oak Grove Elementary

Frequently in my interviews with teachers at City Charter and Oak Grove, I asked teachers to describe what happens on a "good day" in their classroom and what happens on a "bad day." I was curious about how teachers would describe their work—what elements of their work were important enough to contribute to a day that felt successful, as teachers themselves defined it. Teachers' responses frequently included themes related to student engagement and their abilities as teachers to facilitate students' connection to a topic they were learning and to facilitate students' connections with each other:

> When I leave saying that was a good day, I kind of leave, like it's kinda like each lesson, on a lesson-by-lesson, like that was a good lesson, ah, they really got it, you know? Really, it's how much the kids, like how much the kids, like respond to like something that I've taught them and like assignment that they're doing and how that's helping um helping to strengthen their understanding of a concept.—Ms. Robinson, third grade teacher

> For a pretty good day, usually, I won't have any behavior issues. Earlier this week, we had a pretty good day. Everyone turned in their homework. There were not major behavior issues. Everyone's participating and engaged. So, that's a really good day for me. Where it just goes nice and smooth. So, I don't have any major disruptions or anything. Just, everyone's doing what they're supposed to be doing. If they're working in pairs, they're working well, they're collaborating. That's a good day for me.—Ms. Jackson, third grade teacher

> A successful day to me is when they walk out of here happy and smiling. . . . When I see their excitement, like you weren't here to see how Marco looked, but every one of those students looked at those plants, just that excitement in their eyes. They know why it's there, they did it. They own it. It's, they know they're trying to grow lettuce. In math today, just seeing their engagement and

knowing that I was able to walk away, five children voluntarily said, "I want to do this with you" and they went to the back table and we worked together. What they didn't realize, I worked with them for two problems, walked away and was circulating over here, and they looked up, they're like, "Ms. Brown?" I'm like, "See? You didn't need my help." Like, when I can get them to that point, when they think they need it but then you walk away. When what I planned was successful and even more than that, to me that's a successful day. It's not just that all the clips are at the top of the chart, it's what I saw them get out of the lesson.—Ms. Brown, first grade teacher

As the three teachers from Oak Grove shared, successful teaching to them involved the facilitation of students' engagement in learning. The best days of teaching for these teachers involved students' active engagement in learning, seeing students "respond" and "collaborate," seeing "that excitement in their eyes." Ms. Jackson's and Ms. Brown's responses also point to valuing students' ownership along with their learning. Ms. Jackson talked about feeling good when students could work collaboratively together without her intervention. Ms. Brown discussed her enjoyment of being able to assist students with a challenging math assignment and then step away to see them continue the work on their own.

The work that the three teachers are describing is critical to student learning but also not easily measured or standardized. The next chapter explores the role of school reform policies in shaping the interactions between teachers and students at Oak Grove. It examines the ways in which teachers' interactions with students were constrained by requirements to frequently test students and the ways in which the requirements of classroom-wide standardized testing influenced the types of interactional skills that students had the opportunity to learn.

3

"This is the Most
Dreadful Test"

• •

The Hidden Curriculum
of Standardized Testing

On a Thursday morning in December, third grade students are beginning to enter Ms. Jackson's classroom. Ms. Jackson, who identifies as Black and female, is in her fourth year of teaching and first year of teaching at Oak Grove Elementary. Previously, Ms. Jackson taught at a private Christian school in the same county as Oak Grove for three years before transitioning to teach at a public school. Ms. Jackson says she has "always wanted to be a teacher, since [she] was younger." As a child she would play school and teacher, and "when I got to high school, I had this really amazing English teacher, and this really amazing social studies teacher. I was like, 'I love them, I love the effect that they have on their students.' I was like, 'I have to be a teacher.'" Ms. Jackson majored in Elementary Education at a state university and started teaching right after graduation.

At the private school where Ms. Jackson taught, her class sizes ranged from eleven to sixteen students. At Oak Grove, she has a class of twenty-four.

This morning, Ms. Jackson is standing in the doorway of her classroom, greeting each of her twenty-four students as they enter. "Hey, pretty girl," she says. "Who does your hair?" A student who I perceived to be Black and female, her long braids gathered into a large bun on top of her head, enters the classroom. Most students have a paper bag in one hand that I recognize as school breakfast. As students sit down at their desks, they out take a small plastic container of milk, a small carton of what looks like juice, and a shrink-wrapped item that looks like small cookies or small pancakes. The desks in the classroom are arranged in a large three-sided rectangle, similar to a horseshoe shape, with three desks in the middle of the horseshoe.

"Edgar, did I say good morning to you?" Ms. Jackson asks a student whom I perceived to be male and Latino as she walks over to her teacher desk. "No," Edgar says, shaking his head. "Good morning," Ms. Jackson says. "Good morning," Edgar responds. As the students come in, they are hanging up their jackets in a wooden cabinet and placing their book bags on the back of their chairs. The students already in the classroom are eating quietly at their desks. They are wearing variations of the school uniform—navy blue pants or jumpers and white or light blue tops. There is a poster on the chalkboard near the door and next to the classroom rules that says:

MORNING ROUTINE
1 Breakfast (finish and clean up)
2 Hand in your homework
3 Sharpen at least two pencils
4 Complete bellwork assignments
5 When bellwork is complete, you may read independently
6 Prepare your mind for a great day of learning!

By 7:46 A.M., most of the students have arrived, and I can hear the crinkling of wrappers from the school breakfast and quiet talking. Several students are standing in a line at the door with papers in their hands, and Ms. Jackson is marking on her clipboard as she looks through their papers. "You have about thirty seconds to finish," Ms. Jackson says to the class in a low voice. The bell rings at 7:50 A.M. "Alright, guys, let's clean up breakfast," Ms. Jackson says. She checks a few more students' work. "Okay," Ms. Jackson says and calls out three or four students' names. They get up and throw away their breakfast trash.

"Good morning, Oak Grove!" a bright, booming voice says over the PA system. "It is terrific, thankful Thursday. There is no America Counts today." The staff member making announcements leads the students in the Pledge of Allegiance and the School Pledge. After the pledges, there is an announcement about Girl Scouts meeting today. "Juniors 8 to 9. Brownies, Group One, 9 to 9:30 and Brownies, Group Two, 9:30–10," the person reading the announcements says. "Sixth graders are going to camp next week. . . . Let's make sure we are on point for learning today. Teachers, remember the drill at 12:45 today. . . . Remember that this is a learning day and those are our expectations."

"Make sure you hand me your Wednesday folders," Ms. Jackson reminds the students as she walks around the inside of the horseshoe of desks. "And we're starting in 30," she says and starts to count down from thirty in a quiet voice as she continues to check homework. Two students are standing by the sink, sharpening their pencils at the electric pencil sharpener on the counter next to the sink.

"Okay, so here we go," Ms. Jackson says. "The past three days we have been working on area." She reviews what the class has learned so far. "Today, we are going to find an easier way," she explains. The students are quiet and make eye contact with their teacher as she reviews the objectives of the lesson. Two students, Ashley and Natasha, both of whom I perceive to be female and Black, raise their hands. "Let me finish," Ms. Jackson responds. Ashley starts to speak. "Let her finish!" another student says forcefully to Ashley. When Ms. Jackson finishes, Ashley asks for permission to ask the question now. "Yes," Ms. Jackson responds. Ashley starts to say something about the lesson, and Ms. Jackson tells her to wait. "We'll get to that," she adds. Natasha tries to say the same thing, and Ms. Jackson responds in the same way. She asks the students what strategies they used for multiplication. "Arrays," Daniela, who I perceived to be Black and female, shares. "Pictures," Carlos, who I perceived to be male and Latino, answers. "Repeated addition," Alexis, who I perceived to be Black and female, says, as each are called on in succession.

Ms. Jackson stands in front of a projector, which is resting on a table at the front of the room to the left of the screen. She draws a rectangle on a white board that is being projected and labels it eight units by three units. She writes "8 × 3" underneath the shape. "Draw your array for 8 times 3," she instructs the students. She walks around the inside of the horseshoe to point out to students where to draw on the page in their workbook. "Okay, it looks like most of you have it," Ms. Jackson tells the class. She goes back to the projector and draws the array. "Most of you had this," she says. A student corrects her to say that she needs eight rows across rather than down. "I was trying to see if you were awake," Ms. Jackson jokes as she erases her drawing and redraws it. "You can't trick us," a student says. "She tricks us all the time," Carlos corrects.

About seven students are raising a hand, waiting for Ms. Jackson to call on someone to give the answer to a subtraction problem. "24!" Alexis shouts. The classroom is silent, like the students are waiting to see what their teacher will do. "Tell me. What do you think?" Ms. Jackson asks, seeming to decide to ignore Alexis. "Yes!" the students call out, meaning that they agree with her.

Ms. Jackson passes out what look like red counters, placing a pile on each student's desk. "Good job. It looks like you guys got it," she says as she walks around the inside of the horseshoe. The classroom is quiet as she continues passing out the counters. "Alright, guys. It looks good. It looks like you got it," she says. "Can we close our books?" Carlos asks. "In a minute," Ms. Jackson says. She finishes passing out the counters. "Okay, you can close your books," she says. Several students make relieved sounds. "I am going to give you two units," Ms. Jackson says. "You are going to build it with the tiles and then tell me the area."

She draws a rectangle that is six units by three units on the white board that is projected onto the screen at the front of the classroom. The room is quiet as students make the shape with their tiles. "Give me the area using a multiplication sentence," she tells the class. "On the paper?" a student asks quietly. "Yes," Ms. Jackson responds. She walks around and places a small shiny star sticker in students' math journals after she checks the answer and determines it is correct. Most students receive a sticker.

It is 8:37 A.M. "Alright. 30," Ms. Jackson says and starts to count down. "No, Ms. Jackson," students say and raise their hands for her to check their work. Ms. Jackson walks around the classroom, distributing stickers as she counts down. "Okay, what is the area?" Ms. Jackson asks. "18 square units," the students shout out in unison. "Make sure you say square units," the teacher reminds them. Ms. Jackson erases the rectangle on the white board and writes a new problem for the students.

Many of the students have their hands raised with their thumbs up. Ms. Jackson walks around the classroom and places another sticker on the students' papers if they have correctly solved the problem. She begins to count down from thirty as she continues to check the students' work. Ms. Jackson counts down faster at the end. "Okay, we'll do one more," she says, standing at the projector. "No, two more!" a student pleads. "Ten more!" another student says. "I can't write it until you are quiet," Ms. Jackson responds. The class is quiet as the teacher writes a rectangle that is four units by seven units.

"I don't have enough," a student who I perceived to be female says, referring to the number of the tiles on her desk. "Write it out," a student who I perceived to be male tells her. "You can draw it out if you need to," Ms. Jackson tells her. "Improvise," Samantha says. "Impro-?" another student asks, seeming to not have heard the word before. "Improvise means that you make something up with your own self," Samantha, a student who I perceived to be Black and female, who is the classroom's current Fast Math champion, explains matter-of-factly. Ms. Jackson smiles at her, looking impressed. "This is hard," a student says. "You can do it," Ms. Jackson encourages. She counts down from thirty as she continues to check the students' work and distribute stickers. "Two, and I'm coming," Ms. Jackson says to students with their hands still up as she finishes counting down. "Zero," she says as she places a sticker on a student's notebook page. "What's the area of this figure?" Ms. Jackson asks. "Twenty-eight square units," the students shout in unison.

"Okay, one, one more," Ms. Jackson says. "Yay!" several students say. "Try not to use your tiles this time. Draw it out. You can't use tiles on the test," she says. Ms. Jackson draws another rectangle and labels the horizontal line at the top "8 units" and pauses as she decides what to write on the vertical line on the right side of the rectangle. She finally writes "5 units" there. The room is quiet as the students work on the final problem. It sounds like the classroom door is being shaken in its frame several times. "Someone is trying to bust in," a student says. Ms. Jackson looks quizzically at the door. I hear an adult from the hallway say, "Come on," and the noise stops. Mark, a student who I perceived to be Black and male, stands up and starts dancing as Ms. Jackson helps another student. "Go flip your clip," she says to Mark as she looks up.

On the chalkboard next to the projector screen, several pieces of construction paper are laminated together in a long rectangle. Clothespins, one with each student's name on, are clustered on the top green square. The colored pieces of paper say:

Great Job (green)
Warning (orange)
Loss of recess time (lavender)
Phone call home (blue)

Mark walks quietly over to the laminated paper and moves his clothespin down from the green to the orange square. Ms. Jackson starts to count down from thirty. "Ms. Jackson! Ms. Jackson!" two students call out. "Guys, I can see. I can see," she reassures them. The students stop calling to her. Ms. Jackson shakes her head at Daniela who apparently does not have the right answer.

"Remind me what the two strategies are to find the area," Ms. Jackson asks the class when she is finished checking the students' work. "What is the first strategy we use?" "Counting," Omar, a student who I perceived to be Black and male, says. "What do we count?" Ms. Jackson asks. "Squares," Omar responds. "What are those called?" Ms. Jackson asks. "Square units," he says. "Or units squared," Ms. Jackson adds. Ms. Jackson calls on another student to provide the second strategy and the student pauses. "What did we just do?" Ms. Jackson asks. "Multiplication," the student says. Ms. Jackson takes questions from two more students. "Are we experts at area now?" Samantha asks. "Yes, we are experts at area," her teacher confirms.

"You guys did a good job today," Ms. Jackson says to the class. "Thank you," two students say. "Can we get a space high five?" a student asks. Ms. Jackson raises one of her palms as if she is giving half of a high five and several students raise their palms in response, still sitting in their seats. Ms. Jackson gives a real high five to Andre, a small boy who I perceived to be Black and male, who is sitting in the front row of the classroom.

Ms. Jackson asks students to get their social studies books out. It is 9:00 A.M. "What page?" a student asks. "Page 74," Ms. Jackson answers. "Jason is ready. Angeli is ready," Ms. Jackson says. "Okay, while we are waiting for Stephanie, turn and talk to your neighbor. Have you ever moved maybe from one house to another, one country to another, one continent or another, or if you haven't—" The students start to talk to each other. "I'm not finished," Ms. Jackson interjects. Students shush other students who are talking. "Or if you know someone who has moved," Ms. Jackson finishes. The students start talking to each other again. "I moved to Atlanta, to another city," Vanessa, a student who I perceived to be Black and female, says. Ms. Jackson encourages two students to talk to each other, restating her question for them.

"Who has ever moved?" Ms. Jackson asks the whole class after she gets the students' attention. All but one student raises their hands. "Who has ever moved from another country?" she asks, and six students raise their hands. Two students say they moved from El Salvador, one student moved from Guatemala, two moved from Africa, and one from Guyana. "Who has ever moved from another state?" Ms. Jackson asks, and eight students raise their hands. One student moved from California, two from New York, two from Georgia, one from Washington, DC, and one from Virginia. "I moved from—" Ms. Jackson begins. "New York!" several students say.

"Why did you move?" Ms. Jackson asks the students. "It was hard work," Stephanie says. Ms. Jackson asks her a series of questions about what she means until Stephanie describes the hard work her parents had to do in Guatemala to make a living.

"My mom had a new job, and it was too far for her to drive from there," Vanessa says. "So, the commute was too far," Ms. Jackson summarizes.

"We were going to move because there were so many stairs," a student says.

"My mom had my brother, and she wanted to move because it was so violent," Natasha explains.

"We had to move because there were too many bugs and mice," Jason shares.

"Okay," Ms. Jackson says. "So, there wasn't one reason that people move. We all had different reasons," she concludes. "Let's look at page 77. We're talking about moving today."

Edgar begins to read page seventy-seven. A voice comes over the PA and says that the Parent Teacher Association holiday pictures will happen at recess and that if someone took a FedEx box from Ms. Marshall's room in the office, they need to return it. Edgar continues to read.

"How were you feeling when you moved?" Ms. Jackson asks when Edgar finishes. "I was worried that I wouldn't make any friends," Stephanie shares and then names several people in the class in a way that sounds like they are her friends now. Ms. Jackson asks Jason how he felt and stays with him after the boy buries his face in his arm on his desk.

"I cried the whole way here," Vanessa says. "Why?" Ms. Jackson asks. "Because I missed half of my family that I left," she responds. Ms. Jackson says that she was sad to leave the teachers and students at her old school, too.

"I was nervous because I came from a new school, too," she adds. "I was wondering, are the teachers going to like me? Are the kids going to like me?"

Ms. Jackson tells Edgar that he can pick the next reader. Almost all of the students raise their hands. Then Edgar picks Antonio, a student who I perceived to be Latino and male, who is sitting to his left. Antonio reads the next page in the book. Ms. Jackson corrects two of the words he reads.

"Looking at the map, who are some people who came from far away?" she asks, referring to the map in the students' textbook. About eight students raise their hands. Ms. Jackson calls on several students after the first student calls out and then pauses. "Stop calling out," another student says. Ms. Jackson calls on a student who is raising a hand.

"Now we're going to look at the reasons people move, and you can see if it's similar to what we talked about," Ms. Jackson tells the students. Antonio calls on Jaden to read the next section in the textbook. "They're calling on all boys," Tiana, a student who I perceived to be Back and female, protests. Jaden begins to read. Ms. Jackson corrects a few words he struggles with like "opportunity" and "freedom." The students are quiet as he reads, following along in their books, and occasionally helping Jaden with the pronunciation of a word. Jaden lets out a big sigh as he finishes reading and turns around with a big smile to pick the next reader. He chooses another boy to read next.

Ms. Jackson asks the students why the people in the textbook moved and several students answer correctly. "So, this is what we're going to do," Ms. Jackson says. "I'm going to pose a question and then we're going to discuss it, like a debate. Is this a fact or an opinion? Everyone in the U.S. has the opportunity to become whoever he or she wants to be." Most students raise two fingers, indicating that they think it is an opinion.

"So, what do you all think about that?" Ms. Jackson asks the students.

"You can still do it because it's your life and you can do whatever you want as long as you're 18 and over," Tiana says. "Okay," Ms. Jackson responds.

There is a disagreement among a few students about whether the President of the United States can tell you what to do. Most students seem to think that he can.

"No. He's not in control of your body," Tiana argues.

Samantha makes a point that there can be a difference between religion and the law.

"I would protest. Running a protest isn't breaking the law," Tiana asserts.

"Let's get back to the initial question," Ms. Jackson interjects. "And let's hear from some other people."

"I disagree because some people may want to get the same job as another person," Angeli, a student who I perceived to be Latina and female, says.

"Pretend I'm not here," Ms. Jackson says, encouraging the students to talk to each other. "You are having a discussion. Be respectful of each other."

The discussion moves into a debate about whether everyone must have a job. "You all are veering off from my statement," Ms. Jackson says and repeats the statement again.

She calls on another student to contribute. "You are veering off topic again," she says to the student. The discussion continues for another minute or so.

"Okay, so there are two valid points," Ms. Jackson summarizes. "Carlos had a valid point about if you want to do something that is harmful, there are laws against that. Tiana and others have a valid point that you can be a lawyer or policeman. So, that's why this is an opinion: there are two valid points. Okay, we are going to stop here. Today, we talked about why people move and saw that there are some similarities to what we talked about in terms of why we move. Can you save it until next time?" Ms. Jackson asks a student who is raising a hand. "It's time to go to music. Close your social studies books."

The students put their books away in their desks and line up at the door. Ms. Jackson waits until the students are quiet and then walks with them down the hallway. It is 9:42 A.M.

On a "normal" morning, such as this one, Ms. Jackson's classroom is filled with opportunities for students to use their voice, whether it is responding to a math question, reading a portion of a social studies text, sharing their personal experience with moving, participating in a debate, or admonishing a fellow student to follow the classroom rules. Students had both structured and unstructured opportunities to communicate with adults and peers. During the math lesson, students called out for their teacher's attention to make sure that their work would be checked and called out to disrupt the pattern of boys selecting only other boys to read during the social studies lesson.

Ms. Jackson placed some boundaries on students' expression, such as when she paused after a student called out the answer rather than raising a hand or when she asked a student to move their clothespin on the behavior chart for dancing during the lesson. However, overall, students had an active voice in Ms. Jackson's classroom and played a role in enforcing the classroom norms, the duration of an informal assessment (e.g., advocating for additional math questions), and choosing who would read the social studies text next.

By fostering students' autonomy and self-expression, Ms. Jackson was resisting the process of social reproduction identified by Jean Anyon[1] and other scholars that have studied schools serving working-class students. In the 1970s, education scholar Anyon visited five elementary schools in New Jersey over the course of one school year. These five elementary schools served predominately White students of differing social classes—White students from working-class families, middle-class families, affluent professional families, and executive elite families. Anyon observed how teachers taught, disciplined, and evaluated students at each school.

As she analyzed these observations, Anyon found that the work that students were asked to do in each school differed and that these differences closely tracked the work required by employers in each social class. For example, the work that working-class students were asked to do in their schools emphasized following procedures correctly, a skill that is in high demand for working-class jobs like auto repair or building maintenance. In the school serving middle-class children, students were given some choice in how they completed their assignments, with an emphasis on arriving at the right answer, skills that Anyon connected to their parents' work as government workers and accountants. Similarly, the work that students in the executive elite school were asked to do emphasized analytical thinking and embodying authority, skills that were sought after in executive-level positions like the president or general counsel of a corporation.

Through her research, Anyon saw that schools were engaged in a process of social reproduction, teaching students ways of relating to authority and work that would prepare them for employment in the same social class that students' families occupied. She termed this type of learning a "hidden curriculum." In Anyon's words:

> the "hidden curriculum" of schoolwork is tacit preparation for relating to the process of production in a particular way. Differing curricular, pedagogical, and pupil evaluation practices emphasize different cognitive and behavioral skills in each social setting and thus contribute to the development in the children of certain potential relationships to physical and symbolic capital, to authority, and to the process of work. School experience, in the sample of schools discussed here, differed qualitatively by social class. These differences may not only contribute to the development in the children in each social class of certain types of economically significant relationships and not others but would thereby help to reproduce this system of relations in society. In the contribution to the reproduction of unequal social relations lies a theoretical meaning and social consequence of classroom practice.[2]

Importantly, Anyon points out in her definition that the hidden curriculum of schoolwork and the process of social reproduction it supports has consequences both for the lives of individual students and patterns of inequality in larger society. For individual students, the hidden curriculum of schoolwork limits individual students' mobility by restricting access to the types of knowledge and skills that could help working-class students more easily access postsecondary education and middle-class jobs, or middle-class students to navigate a boardroom with more ease. Viewed from a societal perspective, the hidden curriculum of schooling helps to maintain and reinforce existing forms of inequality at a societal level, frustrating the possibility that schools could prepare students for lives and careers of their choosing, that may or may not match the employment trajectories of their parents and grandparents.

In Ms. Jackson's classroom, students were expected to follow particular routines (e.g., the list of preparatory tasks before the school day started), similar to what Anyon found in the working-class schools she visited. However, in Ms. Jackson's classroom, students were also allowed to express their preferences and views and to influence aspects of the math lesson, suggesting that Ms. Jackson's teaching was also resisting the process of social reproduction that Anyon described and offering students a wider array of skills and knowledge they could draw upon.

In a typical lesson, Ms. Jackson also provided many opportunities for informal feedback and evaluation that was different in its structure, compared to the formal, standardized assessments characteristic of school reform policies like NCLB and Race to the Top. Students shared their answers to math questions out loud or by writing them in their notebooks. Students received immediate individual feedback on their work verbally from Ms. Jackson or via the sticker she placed in students' notebooks. The whole class also received feedback as they called out an answer together and received an affirmative response from their teacher or from comments Ms. Jackson would make to the whole class as she reviewed their work, such as "Good job. It looks like you guys got it." At the end of the lesson, Ms. Jackson also provided a summative assessment to her class when a student asked "Are we experts at area now?" Her teacher confirmed that "Yes, we are experts at area." Students completed their work both independently and collectively, quietly and out loud, and received immediate feedback on their progress.

During the lessons, Ms. Jackson provided guideposts for students in terms of their behavior and controlled the flow of the class, letting students know when there were thirty seconds left, when it was time to transition to a new activity, and when it was time to leave the classroom for music. Her demeanor was assertive, encouraging, and kind, reminiscent of the active caring approaches described in culturally relevant approaches to education.

Two main streams of research have emerged within the research on culturally relevant education: culturally responsive teaching and culturally relevant pedagogy.[3] Culturally responsive teaching, as developed by Geneva Gay, includes four aspects—caring, communication, curriculum, and instruction.[4] Caring in the context of culturally responsive teaching is an active form of caring in which teachers set and communicate high expectations for students and work in partnership with students to support students' academic success from a standpoint of "cultural validation and strength."[5]

By studying the practices of teachers who were widely perceived as successful teachers of African American students, Gloria Ladson-Billings developed the theory of culturally responsive pedagogy.[6] Culturally responsive pedagogy includes three components: fostering students' academic achievement, integrating students' culture with academic learning, and developing a critical perspective related to social inequalities. Successful teachers in Ladson-Billings' study took a similarly active caring role in their students' academic achievement, believing that their students were capable of high levels of academic performance and motivating themselves and their students to meet those expectations.[7] Teachers created "equitable and reciprocal" relationships with their students, valued students' cultural knowledge and expertise, and created conditions where students were expected to take responsibility for the success of not just themselves but the other students in their classroom.[8]

In her classroom, Ms. Jackson embodied many of the dimensions of this "active caring" approach. She communicated her care for students as soon as her students entered the classroom, by greeting each student by name. She held high expectations for students during lessons and encouraged them to meet these expectations. During the math lesson, when a student expressed "This is hard," Ms. Jackson followed up with an encouraging statement: "You can do it." During the debate, she frequently encouraged students to meet her expectations of communicating peer-to-peer and staying on topic with a prompt. In an interview, Ms. Jackson described what students' families value about her teaching in terms of her high expectations for her students: "I've heard, they like that I'm kind of tough on them. I don't tolerate mediocre stuff because I'm like when you get to the next grade and you're still doing this mediocre, you're going to keep falling farther and farther behind. So, I'm really stuck on little stuff. And they might think it's real minute and real small but I'm like it's really important when you get higher on in your education. So, they like that I'm kind of hard on them."

Combined with her high expectations, Ms. Jackson also demonstrated empathy and an awareness of students' social and emotional needs. During the social studies lesson, she provided space for students to discuss how they felt about moving and allowed students to express a range of emotions, including worry and sadness. When Jason seemed upset during the discussion, burying his face in his arm, Ms. Jackson lent her physical and emotional presence as a support. In doing so, Ms. Jackson provided opportunities for students to articulate how they felt about a significant moment in their lives, to hear and support other students' feelings and experiences, and provided support for students who were having a tough time being with or sharing their experience. Several of the students' responses pointed to the experience of trauma related to poor housing conditions or violence, underscoring the adverse psychological and emotional effects related to economic disadvantage.[9] The ability to respond empathetically and to develop meaningful relationships with students are two key competencies in trauma-informed education, competencies that Ms. Jackson embodied in her teaching.[10]

Across my observations in Ms. Jackson's classroom, there were numerous examples of the results of Ms. Jackson fostering "equitable and reciprocal" relationships of mutual respect. Students frequently "shushed" other students who were talking over Ms. Jackson, demonstrating their respect for her. Rather than responding negatively when Jaden struggled with reading the social studies passage, students helped him with difficult words. When talking about what students appreciate about her teaching, Ms. Jackson says, "They feel comfortable coming to me because they know I don't tolerate a lot of disrespect towards each other, so they feel real comfortable in the classroom. I think those things are really, really important for learning and development."

Finally, as pedagogues, culturally responsive educators value students' cultural knowledge and expertise and design classroom activities that engage different communication styles, patterns of task engagement, and student experiences. In her math lesson, Ms. Jackson used a variety of instructional strategies, from having students call out answers to allowing students to work independently and at their own pace on practice questions. Ms. Jackson spent time contextualizing the social studies lesson by allowing students to share their personal experiences with moving and their personal beliefs about the debate topic. It was also clear that Ms. Jackson had incorporated her own personal history into the classroom, when she started to share where she had moved from, and students began to answer for her. These practices emerged organically in Ms. Jackson's classroom. They were part of the folk knowledge and skills in cultural responsiveness Ms. Jackson brought to her classroom and allowed her to personalize students' learning.

In the context of closing achievement gaps, the stated aim of school reform policies, Ms. Jackson is engaging in many of the practices that education researchers characterize as elements of culturally relevant education. She is communicating high expectations for students while demonstrating care and respect for her students. And she is teaching in ways that engage students' voices and experiences in the curriculum. In Ms. Jackson's classroom, these strategies helped to foster students' engagement with academic work, whether it was learning about how to find the area of an object or learning about why people move as part of a social studies lesson.

The different patterns of communication and engagement that Ms. Jackson offered in her classroom—working independently on a math assignment, calling out responses, negotiating with a teacher over the number of additional math problems assigned, and debating fellow students as part of a social studies lesson—allowed students to learn and practice different styles of communication that crossed the boundaries of interactional styles associated with different social classes. Students were learning to follow directions, communicate and negotiate with those in authority, and make and defend arguments to their peers. Students had the opportunity to connect and converse with peers from diverse backgrounds, which offered the chance to expand their cultural and linguistic capital. Far from engaging in a simple process of social reproduction, Ms. Jackson was offering her students a chance to cultivate skills they could use in a variety of educational and employment settings.

Testing Day

About a week and a half later, the normal rhythm of Ms. Jackson's classroom gave way to a standardized testing day.

On this morning, there are eight students already in the classroom, sitting at their desks and eating school breakfast. The school breakfast today is a small plastic container of milk, a small carton of juice, and what looks like a small pancake, all packaged in a brown paper bag. "Nine days until Christmas," Carlos says. "Andre, do you have a note from Friday?" Ms. Jackson asks. "What? I'll get one tomorrow," Andre responds, in what may be a reference to a recent absence. "Tiana, I am not going to wait for you to get it together this morning," Ms. Jackson says in a warning tone, directing her comment toward the back right corner of the classroom, where Tiana is seated. The students' homework is projected on the screen at the front of the classroom. It says:

Reading	Log, writing a play
Spelling	Neatly in pen
Math	p. 763

"You guys have a couple minutes left to finish breakfast," Ms. Jackson says at 7:42 A.M. "You guys have one minute left. Start cleaning up if you're finished." Several students stand up and throw their breakfast bags away. "Alright, let's start cleaning up. The bell's about to ring," Ms. Jackson says. Several students stay seated, eating their breakfast. "By the time I come back, breakfast needs to be finished, and you need to have your homework copied," Ms. Jackson says. The bell rings at 7:50 A.M.

Mr. Paulson, who I perceived to be White and male and who was one of the school support staff members, stands just inside the door. Students talk quietly as they finish their breakfast, sharpen pencils, and write their homework down in their agenda notebooks. At 7:53 A.M., a voice comes over the PA: "Please stand for the Pledge of Allegiance." The students stand and recite the pledge along with the person reading the announcements. "Oak Grove staff member of the month," the voice continues. Two different voices come over the PA, possibly teachers: "Reading Resource Teacher Ms. Buchanan for being a good collaborator." The original voice comes back on and continues with the remainder of the announcements: "All donations for holiday bags to the ESOL room Wednesday. Any desks that are not being used by students, put [them] in the hallway. I realize that you use these for other things but we really need desks at this point. . . . Instrumental music schedule: 10:15 . . . Basketball practice at 2:15 today. . . . Holiday pictures at recess. . . . Thank you. . . . Have a great day."

It is 8:13 A.M. The students are talking loudly to each other as Mr. Paulson stands in front of the room. Samantha pushes Tiana back toward her seat. "Sit. Sit. Sit. Don't fight with him," she says to Tiana. Tiana pokes the boy sitting next to her, and Mr. Paulson comes over and says something to them. "Ms. Jackson's class. You are too noisy. You can get a book to read until she comes back," he says. All the students get up and head toward the library. The students cluster around the plastic bins of books in the library.

Ms. Jackson comes back into the room at 8:17 A.M. "Okay, no talking starts now. Everything away," she says to the class. "Do not write on the book. Do not write on the book. Say it with me 'do not write on the book.'" The students repeat the instruction with her. "Do not write on the book," Ms. Jackson says again as she begins to pass out the test booklets. "Roberto, do you have your glasses? Mark, stop talking. Why is there paper on the floor already?" Ms. Jackson asks as she passes by Andre's desk. Andre draws the paper toward him with his foot and then picks it up.

Ms. Jackson finishes passing out the booklets. "Do you need to flip your clip already this morning?" she asks Mark. "No," he says. Ms. Jackson passes out pencils to students. "Close your book. I did not tell you to open it," she says to Mark. "Does everyone have a pencil?" "Yes," several students say in quiet voices. "Bubble in your name and write your name where it says here," Ms. Jackson instructs the students and passes out the answer sheets. She walks over to the door with a red piece of paper with typed text that says "Testing . . ." on it and puts it on the front of the door.

"Does everyone have a test booklet? Does everyone have an answer sheet? Does everyone have a pencil?" Ms. Jackson asks the class in a quiet tone that sounds tired or frustrated or both.

"Yes," several students say in a quiet tone.

"Okay, open to the first page. Follow along as I read the directions," she instructs and reads the first direction in the test booklet. "You are filling in your answer on the answer sheet," she repeats twice.

"This is just like our practice on Friday," she tells the students. "Don't rush but don't take forever, obviously."

"Are we going to have math after this?" Tiana asks.

"Don't worry about that right now," Ms. Jackson responds. "Take your time because when you are finished, you can't do anything. You can't read. You can't draw. Any more questions? Alright, you can start."

The classroom is quiet as students look down at their test booklets and mark on their answer sheets. It is 8:28 A.M. Ms. Jackson stands at the desk with the projector on it and types on a laptop with her back to the class. A student draws in a breath sharply, and Ms. Jackson turns and scans the classroom before turning back around to the laptop. Ms. Jackson puts a stack of papers on her desk and then stands at the front of the class and writes something on a piece of paper.

A voice comes over the PA: "Ms. Marshall, please come to the main office. Ms. Marshall, please report to the main office."

Ms. Jackson walks over to Emmanuel, who is sitting next to Tiana, and gives him a different paper. "Choose one," she says to him, pointing at the paper. "Pick one."

Ms. Jackson stops by where I am sitting at the back of the classroom to tell me that the students are taking a reading test to determine their grade level in reading. The test is from the county. The students first took the test in August, so this is their second time taking it. "Basic context clues," Ms. Jackson explains. She adds that Emmanuel has to take the test, even though he recently moved to Oak Grove and speaks French but not very much English.

Ms. Jackson walks around the right side of the horseshoe, looking down at a student's paper. She whispers something to two students, walks inside the horseshoe, and then goes back to the front of the room. She takes a sip out of a large plastic cup that looks like it might have iced coffee in it.

Ms. Jackson adjusts Tiana's divider. "I need you to sit up at your desk," she says twice quietly. Tiana is sitting with her feet on her chair and her test on her thighs, her knees against the front of her desk. Tiana unfolds her long legs and puts the test on her desk. Several moments later, she puts her winter coat that was on the back of her chair over her white short-sleeved t-shirt. At least one other student is wearing a coat while taking the test. The rest of the students are wearing zip-up sweatshirts of various colors or long-sleeved shirts under their polos or jumpers.

Tiana is standing at her desk. "Sit," Ms. Jackson says in a loud whisper, and Tiana sits down. She is wearing glasses with thick purple plastic frames. About a minute later, Tiana stands and takes a Hello Kitty backpack with a black and white snakeskin pattern and places it on the back of her chair. Ms. Jackson walks over to her and tells her in a quiet tone that she can't be moving around so much during the test. Tiana sits down and a few minutes later, she is back sitting with her knees up and her test booklet on her thighs.

Ms. Jackson stands at the front of the room and then walks over to the right side of the room. The classroom's heater roars to life. Ms. Jackson walks to the left inside the horseshoe, looks down at Mark's work, and then stands at the front of the room looking from one side of the room to the other. It is 8:45 A.M. On the chalkboard, the class schedule has "B week" written next to it. The schedule, written in chalk, says:

Breakfast	7:30–7:50	Morning Meeting	10:25–10:50
Math	8–9	Recess	10:50–11:10
Social Studies	9–9:40	Lunch	11:10–11:35
PE	9:40–10:25	Reading	11:35–1:40

Ms. Jackson walks over to Tiana and explains quietly why she needs to sit up at her desk. "If someone comes in and sees . . ." Ms. Jackson says, indicating Tiana's test booklet is outside her divider. Tiana pushes her chair in, and Ms. Jackson adjusts her divider. Ms. Jackson walks over to the heater and places five large paperback textbooks on top of it, possibly to muffle the loud sound emanating from the heater. "I'm finished," Alex, a student who I perceived to be Latino and male, says in a quiet voice. "There is no way you should be finished," Ms. Jackson says from the front of the room in a voice loud enough for most of the class to hear. About a minute later, Alex scoots his chair closer to his desk loudly several times.

Ms. Jackson stands at the front of the room, looking from one side to the other, and then crouches by a student's desk and says something in a low tone. She walks back to the front of the room and takes a sip of her iced coffee and then walks along the right side of the horseshoe of desks. It is 8:54 A.M. Ms. Jackson picks up the clipboard that she was holding earlier and places it on her desk. She walks to the opposite side of the room to a set of shelves, picks up a packet of looseleaf paper, and takes a sheet out. She puts the pack of papers back and stands at the front of the classroom, writing on the clipboard.

Tiana stretches back in her chair. The classroom is quiet, except for the heater and the occasional paper rustling or foot kicking lightly against a metal chair leg. Ms. Jackson is still writing quickly on the clipboard. She looks up at the students, and there is a sound of a quiet burp. Ms. Jackson scans the room with a slightly irritated look on her face and then goes back to writing on the paper on the clipboard.

At 9:00 A.M., Ms. Jackson stops writing and takes the paper off the clipboard. She places it on the projector desk, takes a sip of the iced coffee, and then walks around the inside of the horseshoe. "Put that back," she says softly to Emmanuel and puts up a divider for a girl who had it lying flat on her desk. Ms. Jackson walks back to the front of the room and then returns to Emmanuel. "Put that away, okay?" she whispers to him and then goes back to the front of the classroom. She picks up a mini white board with a yellow paper on it and writes something on it in black marker.

A student sneezes. "Bless you," about five students say. The first few seem serious; the last two, less so. Ms. Jackson puts down the white board, marker, and yellow paper on the desk with the projector on it. "You are finished?" she asks Mark quietly from the front of the room. Mark nods. "You checked your work?" Ms. Jackson asks. Mark nods. "All 45 of them?" she asks him twice, seeming skeptical. "You went back to read all 45 of them and all the passages?" she repeats. Mark nods, and Ms. Jackson doesn't say anything else.

There is a loud beep from the PA. Emmanuel is sitting with his chin on his desk. The rest of the students are sitting up and most appear to be still working on their test—their booklets are open, and they are looking down at them.

At 9:11 A.M., Ms. Jackson walks over to two students whose desks face the front row and looks down at their work, her facial expression remaining neutral. She continues to walk around the inside of the horseshoe.

"You guys have time to check your work. Instead of just sitting there, I would go back to make sure I have all 45 correct. And then, I would go back and check again," Ms. Jackson urges the class. It is 9:20 A.M. Kira, a student who I perceive to be Black and female, stands up. "You're not leaving," Ms. Jackson tells her. Kira turns and takes something out of her backpack. Ms. Jackson tells her to put her divider back up.

Ms. Jackson walks over to the shelves and picks up a pack of computer paper. She takes out a sheet and puts the pack back on top of a stack of what looks like three unopened stacks of plain white computer paper. She walks to the front of the room, puts the paper on the clipboard, and writes on it with a pen while facing the class. Kira has a plastic container with some type of orange drink on her desk. Ms. Jackson walks over and taps on Angeli's desk. "Get up," Ms. Jackson says and tells Angeli to check her work. Ms. Jackson walks back to the front of the room and continues to write on her clipboard quickly. Every so often, she looks up at the students.

At 9:26 A.M., Ms. Jackson places what looks like a finished handwritten letter on the projector desk. She walks the inside of the horseshoe of desks before returning to the front of the room and writing on the clipboard again. Ms. Jackson walks over to her teacher desk and picks up something that looks like a small bottle of whiteout. She shakes the bottle, twists the top off, applies some of it to the paper on the clipboard, and then starts writing again. There are learning objectives written in chalk next to different colored sentence strips with subjects written on them in black marker. They say:

Reading: Students will identify parts of a play.
Social Studies: Students will discuss ways cultural groups are alike and
    different.
Math: Students will use various strategies to find the area of a
    figure.
Science/Health: Students will compare different kinds of minerals.
Writing: Students will explain different perspectives and write entries
    from different points of view.
Spelling: Prefixes—re, und, dis, mis
Bringing Words to Life: abundant, existence, scarce
Question of the Week: How do people explain things in nature?

It is 9:34 A.M. Ms. Jackson places what looks like a second handwritten note on the projector desk along with the clipboard and pen. She walks along the right side of the horseshoe. She stops at Andre's desk at the front of the room and whispers something to him. It sounds like she might be redirecting him. She does the same for a student sitting two desks away from him.

Ms. Jackson says something quietly to Samantha, and Samantha walks to the right side of the room, lifts a metal panel, and flips a switch. The rumbling of the heater stops. Ms. Jackson places the test materials into a yellow plastic bin resting on an empty desk at the front of the room and then collects students' pencils, placing them in a white letter-sized envelope. Two students still have test booklets on their desks. "Do you want to flip your clip?" Ms. Jackson asks Andre. "You too," she says to Joshua. "This is why I don't put you next to each other because you don't know how to act," she says. Ms. Jackson is at the front of the room, reading something in a manila folder with her last name written on it in large green letters. Tiana taps on her desk. Mark bounces his body in his chair.

It is 9:50 A.M. Ms. Jackson picks up the test booklets from the students' desks at the front of the room. "Finished?" she asks Carlos and looks back when she hears a noise behind her. She turns back and then looks back again when there is a louder noise—a chair or desk scraping against the floor. "Elena, please," she says firmly. Ms. Jackson hands a divider that had fallen to Elena who made the loud noise because she was leaning over her desk, trying to reach the folder.

Ms. Jackson types on a laptop, her fingernails making a clicking sound against the keyboard. She writes something on a piece of paper while looking at the laptop screen. The students are quiet. Several have their heads down on their desks. Tiana is doing what looks like a quiet step routine at her desk. "There is too much movement. Be still," Ms. Jackson says, holding up a palm in a "stop" motion toward the direction of the sound of a chair scraping. The classroom is so quiet that I can hear the sound of the sink dripping. Ms. Jackson counts the test booklets she is holding in her arm and then places them in the yellow plastic bin. She leans back against the projector desk, looking at the students.

It is now 9:57 A.M. Ms. Jackson walks back to me. "With this test, I can't stop until everyone is done, and this is their specials time. It's my break time but I can't stop until everyone is done," she whispers to me.

Ms. Jackson walks back to the front of the room and looks up at the ceiling, shifting her weight from one leg to the other. Ms. Jackson is swaying back and forth with her hands on her hips, a frustrated look on her face. I am amazed at the students' ability to stay quiet for this long with nothing to do. "Alright, line up for specials," Ms. Jackson says at 10:04 A.M. as she takes a test booklet from Alicia, the last student taking the test. The students get up quickly and walk into the hallway. Ms. Jackson leaves with them and then comes right back into the room.

"This is the most dreadful test," she says when she returns. "There are no accommodations. They can't have books out. They can't leave until all are finished." A student comes back in to say that the PE (physical education) teacher isn't there. Ms. Jackson leaves briefly and then comes back in with a sigh. She tells me that the students were supposed to take the test last Wednesday, but school was closed due to snow on Tuesday, and they didn't want to do it the day after a snow day. Then, on Thursday, the school didn't have enough test booklets for all of the third grade, so Ms. Jackson's class didn't take the test. Then, the school's assistant principal was absent on Friday, so they couldn't test then. Today, Ms. Jackson says, the assistant principal was supposed to open testing at 7:00 A.M. but she didn't arrive until the announcement on the PA stated that testing was open. "I could have started earlier," Ms. Jackson says, sounding frustrated.

The "dreadful test" that Ms. Jackson was implementing was a standardized reading test that was administered quarterly at the school. The test was "high stakes" in that the results would be used to determine resources that students would be able to access. The test determined which students would be classified as "below grade level," "on grade level," and "above grade level." Students deemed below grade level were offered the opportunity to access free tutoring services after school. The test was also one of three tests used to determine per pupil funding levels for the school the following year. The end-of-year state assessment would determine funding levels for third through fifth grade students, while the standardized reading test the students had just taken would determine funding levels for second grade students. For each student designated as "below grade level" or "above grade level," the school would receive extra funding to provide targeted educational resources for those students.

The administration of the test affected the autonomy Ms. Jackson had to control her teaching schedule for the day and shaped the types of interactions she had with students. As Ms. Jackson described after the test, she had little control over when the test would be administered and how long it would take the students to complete. The requirements that all students had to remain seated, quiet, and without alternate assignments until all of their classmates finished meant that Ms. Jackson was unable to tell Tiana at the beginning of class whether the math lesson would happen that morning or not.

The interactional style that characterized Ms. Jackson's communications with her students on a testing day stood in sharp contrast to how Ms. Jackson normally engaged with her students. The reciprocal call and response nature of Ms. Jackson's math lesson on a "normal" classroom day was replaced with a more directive one-way form of communication in which students were asked to comply with nonnegotiable instructions and to remain quiet while doing so. Ms. Jackson's role became one of enforcing these norms of behavior, including the norm for students to sit still, as she reinforced several times with Tiana, who was normally one of the most active and vocal students in class. The process of standardized testing in Ms. Jackson's classroom emphasized that students passively follow directions and procedures, pointing to a hidden curriculum for this type of testing, as it emphasized skills associated with working-class jobs. While there were small instances of resistance from some students (e.g., making noise, moving around), these actions placed students at risk of being disciplined by their teacher, rather than opening up opportunities for different types of interactions. Students' self-expression and even their ability to move their body into a more comfortable position was limited or discouraged as part of the need to demonstrate proper testing procedure.

The Hidden Curriculum of Standardized Testing

As the examples from Ms. Jackson's classroom demonstrate, mastering academic skills and content is only a part of the learning that students engage in within schools. Students are also expected to learn the behaviors and habits that will allow them to be successful students, as defined by their schools. At Oak Grove Elementary, standardized testing requirements played a significant role in structuring interactions between students and teachers and in the types of noncognitive skills that were transmitted to students. Standardized testing played such a significant role in shaping interaction at Oak Grove due to an intersecting set of conditions that included the frequency with which tests were administered, the high stakes nature of the tests, and the amount of surveillance that teachers and students were subject to at the school.

During my observations at Oak Grove Elementary, students were frequently engaged in some form of assessment or preparing for an assessment. These assessments were designed to meet requirements set by the school, the school district, and the federal government. At the school level, teachers were required to input a certain number of student grades each week in an online system that was accessible to students' parents. On weeks with four or five days of school, teachers were required to post two grades for each subject. On weeks with fewer days of school, teachers were required to post one grade for each subject. And even during a week when students were out of school for all but one day due to inclement weather, teachers were informed that they were still expected to submit one grade for each subject. As a result, and to inform their own instruction, teachers regularly assessed students' mastery of certain subjects including spelling, reading, writing, math, social studies, and science.

At the district level, teachers in second grade and above were required to give students a standardized reading assessment four times per year to track students' progress in meeting the goal of reading on or above grade level. As part of the new teacher evaluation system, implemented by the school district with funding from the federal Race to the Top grant, teachers had to choose their own Student Learning Objectives to assess and track. The teacher evaluation system also required students to complete a survey about their classroom experiences, which was implemented by a school district staff member. Students in the English as a Second Language program, approximately 40 percent of students at Oak Grove Elementary, completed a standardized test to determine their future placement in the program.

At the federal level, teachers were in the process of transitioning to the new federal Common Core requirements. This meant that teachers were in the process of preparing students for the end-of-year state assessment (the standardized test that would demonstrate whether the school met existing federal accountability requirements) and for the PARCC (Partnership for Assessment of Readiness for College and Careers) test that would replace the state assessment the following year. In nearly every observation I conducted at Oak Grove, students were engaged during at least a portion of the school day in an assessment, and I often heard teachers reminding students at the end of the school day about an upcoming test.

As teachers prepared students for the many assessments they would encounter during the school year and implemented those assessments, they taught (sometimes implicitly and sometimes explicitly) skills that would help students to be successful test-takers. These skills included many of the tasks scholars have associated with working-class employment, including following directions, working quietly and independently, and limiting movement. The sections that follow demonstrate that these skills were taught widely across classrooms at Oak Grove as part of the school's work to meet school reform requirements.

Following Directions

"Can you come and get these?" Ms. Jackson asks. Several students in her third grade classroom walk over to where Ms. Jackson is standing by the left side of the classroom and pick up red and yellow workbooks that say "Ready Common Core" on the front. Ms. Jackson walks back to a c-shaped table at the back of the classroom and sits behind it. The students in the first group join her. "Where is your readers response notebook?" Ms. Jackson asks Joshua. "I never had one," Joshua replies. "What have you been doing this whole year?" she asks him. "Using paper," Joshua says, squirming a bit. "Okay, get a piece of paper," Ms. Jackson says, and Joshua goes to a shelf and takes a piece of looseleaf paper.

"Okay, page 171," Ms. Jackson says to the group. "Follow along as I read. Page 171." Ms. Jackson begins to read from the workbook and then pauses. "What should you do before you read the passage?" she asks the group.

Ms. Jackson calls on Angeli. "The title," Angeli says. "No, before that," Ms. Jackson responds and calls on Oscar. "The directions," Oscar answers. "Yes, Oscar, the directions," Ms. Jackson confirms. "Yeah, Oscar!" Joshua affirms. "Read the directions," Ms. Jackson says to Oscar, and he reads the directions written in the workbook.

Most assessments and practice assessments I observed at Oak Grove began with the teacher emphasizing the importance of reading and following the directions of the test. The directions included: how to answer the questions, including how to complete any separate answer sheets for the test; whether a student could write in a test booklet or not; and the specific elements that students needed to include in their answers. These skills needed to be mastered in order for students' knowledge to be accurately measured by the test. Misunderstanding the instructions or how to transfer an answer to an answer sheet could result in a student appearing not to have learned a particular skill or content area.

Each test that students took—whether school-based or required by the school district or federal government—had a different format, so students had to learn a different set of directions for each assessment. A common instruction from teachers and question from students was whether students could write in the test booklet or not, and the answer varied based on the assessment.

"In your best handwriting, write your first and last names on the answer sheet," Ms. Robinson instructs her third grade class on a morning in December. The students are quiet as they begin to write. Two students at each table have a blue divider up that extends around three sides of their desks.

"I am going to pass out this test booklet. Do not write in it. I repeat: Do not write in the test booklet. I repeat again: Do not write in the test booklet," Ms. Robinson repeats with more emphasis each time. "Does anyone have a question about that?"

"Are we allowed to write on the answer sheet?" Michael asks, after raising a hand and receiving permission to speak.

"Yes. Thank you for asking about that," Ms. Robinson replies.

Sofia raises a hand and asks something quietly. "No, we're not going to use the brain space below," Ms. Robinson answers. "This isn't a math test. You won't have to take notes."

Ms. Robinson explains to her students why they are not going to write in the test booklet: Dr. Sanders, the assistant principal, says it's difficult to send the test booklets back to get new ones if students write in them. Ms. Robinson asks students to bubble in the circle next to their names on the left side of the answer sheet. After all of the students give her a thumbs up to indicate they have done this, she tells them that they can begin the test and that they will be working on the whole test at their own pace.

In this instance, Ms. Robinson's class was preparing to take a quarterly standardized reading assessment required by their school district. The school district only had a certain number of test booklets, so each third grade class had to take the test on a different day, and students had to be instructed not to write in the test booklet so that they would be available for the next class. By halfway through their third grade year, students were familiar enough with the procedure of testing to know that they should ask about whether it is appropriate to write on the answer sheet and whether they should be using space on the answer sheet to work out their answers. In response to the latter question, Ms. Robinson provides some guidance on differentiating between math and reading assessments—math assessments might require calculations that would require the use of the "brain space below," while reading assessments shouldn't require the use of notes.

In contrast, a little less than two months later, Ms. Robinson's class is learning how to take tests in the format required by the school district's math assessment, which was preparing students for the transition to the Common Core curriculum. Ms. Robinson passes out a test to each student. "Go ahead and write your name on it," she says twice as she moves around the room. "Take your time. Do the best you can. Read everything carefully." The students begin to write on the test papers. The classroom is quiet. "Boys and girls, you can absolutely write on this paper. You can write numbers, symbols . . . anything you need to do to find the answer," Ms. Robinson instructs.

Later, after students have completed the test and attended a school assembly, Ms. Robinson takes time to make sure students understand how to transfer their responses to the answer sheet that is specific to this test.

"I am going to pass back your tests and show you how to write the answers and then we will do writing and if we have time, science," Ms. Robinson tells the class. She passes the math tests back to the students while a student, Sonia, who I perceived to be Latina and female, passes out a blank answer sheet to each student. "There is no talking," Ms. Robinson reminds the students. "If you are, I will assume the worst. And that is that you are cheating." The students are quiet as the tests are passed out. "Okay, now, boys and girls, we will fill out the answer sheet. Do me a favor and write with your neatest handwriting your first and last name. And then go over to the left and bubble in your name," she says. The students begin writing on their answer sheets.

"Now, so whatever numbers you bubbled in for one, two, three, and four, please bubble it in on your answer sheet," Ms. Robinson instructs. A student sighs. The teacher repeats the instruction. "Once you have done numbers one, two, three, and four, I want you to write down the number for number five. The area . . . for number six, I want you to write down the answer you believe is correct," Ms. Robinson says. She tells Julia, who I perceived to be Latina and female, how to write the two numbers separated by a comma for the answer to number six. Ms. Robinson guides the students how to write the remaining five or six answers on their answer sheets. "Once you are finished . . . ," she says and then tells the students how to place their answer sheets and their tests on their desks and says she will collect them.

As demonstrated above, the curriculum of testing at Oak Grove Elementary included mastering a set of skills related to the practice of test taking, including the ability to follow directions and to differentiate between the directions for different types of standardized tests. In some cases, this was taught explicitly by teachers. In other cases, students were reminded to follow the directions and expected to follow the correct procedures themselves. Across a wide variety of assessments, students were repeatedly prompted to follow the test's directions exactly as they were stated, without deviating from the procedures for a particular test, whether that was writing directly on the test (or not) or following the norms of a particular answer sheet. Deviating from these norms could lead to an incorrect answer, a test booklet that could no longer be used in a context of scarce resources, and dismay or discipline from a teacher.

In Ms. Phillips' second grade classroom, Ms. Kaufman, an English for Speakers of Other Languages (ESOL) teacher who I perceived to be White and female, is meeting with a group of students to administer a practice test. "I noticed that this ESOL student listened and paid attention. This one did. This ESOL student did," Ms. Kaufman says as she looks down at her group's work. "The teacher can only say this once during a listening test," Ms. Kaufman reminds the students and seems to be directing this comment particularly to a student in her group who didn't follow directions.

A few minutes later, the silence in the classroom is broken by a loud sound. "Uh!" Ms. Kaufman says sharply in a "stop" tone. Ms. Phillips looks over toward the ESOL group. Ms. Kaufman seems to realize that her voice was loud enough for the lead teacher to hear across the classroom and looks a bit embarrassed. "Someone wrote on the workbook," she explains.

Working Quietly and Independently

Assessments were also typically completed in silence and teachers strongly emphasized the need for students to work quietly and independently on their test.

In Ms. Robinson's classroom, the students are preparing for a math test. "Three, two, one. I am passing out test materials, so it needs to be quiet. Who needs to move their name?" Ms. Robinson asks, referring to the classroom's behavior chart, when she hears a student still talking. Ms. Robinson passes out blue dividers from a box, giving one to every other student at each desk cluster. The students begin to talk again. "I asked you all to be quiet. I will not ask again," Ms. Robinson says in a louder, firmer tone. I don't hear any students talking after this.

In some cases, as with the test Ms. Robinson was implementing above, teachers had to remind students explicitly that talking was not allowed during the assessment. In other cases, students practiced this skill without prompting.

Ms. Jackson walks to the front of the room. "Okay, make sure you are writing in complete sentences with punctuation and capitalization and make sure you are answering what the question is asking," she tells the class. Students have dividers up around their desks, and Ms. Jackson passes out the tests one by one to the students. "You can start once you get your test," she says. The class is quiet as the students write on their tests—a single sheet, double-sided.

Working quietly and independently was seen as evidence that students were following the rules of testing and not cheating on the assessment. (Recall Ms. Robinson's admonition to her students during the math practice assessment—"There is no talking," Ms. Robinson reminds the students. "If you are, I will assume the worst. And that is that you are cheating.")

Working independently on assessments was also enforced symbolically across classrooms by the use of dividers—three-sided cardboard boards that protected a student's test from the view of other students.

In Ms. Phillips' second grade classroom, her co-teacher, Ms. Gonzales is preparing the students for a spelling test. "You're not following directions," Ms. Gonzales says three times as she passes out orange and red folders to the students. The students stand the folders up on their desk like they are dividers. "We are going to take our spelling test," Ms. Phillips says and begins to pass out blank looseleaf pieces of paper.

Dividers were used across classrooms at Oak Grove Elementary when students were taking assessments. They protected students' work from the gaze of other students and also symbolically and practically did the work of isolating students from each other, helping to ensure that students' work was completed quietly and independently.

Along with limiting students' gaze and communication, standardized tests required a particular curriculum of the body,[11] namely, that students did not move from their seats for the duration of the test. The image of students sitting still and quietly helped classes to produce evidence that they were testing in the "correct way"—that the environment was conducive to working quietly and independently and that students were being held responsible for producing their own work without communication or assistance from other students. The amount that students were required to sit still varied by the length of the test and could last as long as a few hours, in the case of the test in Ms. Jackson's classroom described above.

Taken together, these examples demonstrate that standardized tests at Oak Grove were not simply doing the work of producing outcomes to support an audit-driven culture of education: They were also doing the work of transmitting a particular set of interactional styles and skills that are associated with working-class employment, including deferring to authority and following directions. The sheer amount of testing requirements that teachers and students faced at Oak Grove meant that the hidden curriculum of standardized testing played a significant role in structuring the interactions between teachers and students and the (lack of) interactions between students and each other. The amount of time students spent engaged in testing limited the time students had to develop other types of interactional skills, including negotiating with those in authority and working collaboratively with peers. It also introduced another layer of control and surveillance of students' bodies, as students were required to sit quietly for long periods of time in ways that demonstrated proper testing procedures. The two chapters that follow examine another set of interactional patterns shaped by school reform policies, particularly the relative level of autonomy from surveillance afforded to City Charter and the ample time and resources that the school devoted to implementing restorative practices. These practices provided students with many opportunities to learn interactional skills associated with middle-class institutions but frequently lacked a focus on the culturally responsive education that students had access to in Ms. Jackson's class.

Part 3

City Charter School

• •

4

Working as Part of a
School Reform Movement
•••••••••••••••••••••••

Urgency, Achievement Gaps,
and Individual Responsibility

On a Tuesday morning in late May, I arrive at City Charter School. City Charter is located in a city in the mid-Atlantic region of the United States. The school was founded in the early 2000s during a period of rapid gentrification. As Black working-class families were displaced, more White middle-class families moved to the neighborhood and were more likely to send their children to City Charter than to the neighborhood public school. During the year that I observed, City Charter served a student population that was 43 percent Black/African American, 17 percent White, and 32 percent Latino/Hispanic. More than half (60 percent) of students were eligible for free and reduced meals.

City Charter had ample resources to meet students' needs. City Charter School was proposed and founded with financial support from a private non-profit organization that provided resources to plan the school and assist with the rental of the first space that housed the school. During its first decade of operation, connections to school reform networks and private foundations allowed school administrators to grow City Charter's enrollment and staffing and to provide an extended school day and school year to students. The school employed a full-time school nurse and school social worker, and teachers had access to a wide range of supplies and instructional materials to support their work. However, as this chapter will demonstrate, these resources combined with a particular structure and culture of work related to school reform policies did not always translate into creating a sustainable working environment for teachers.

I've arrived earlier than usual at City Charter, and the school is quiet. It will be about another twenty minutes before the rush of parents and students that occurs in the five to ten minute window around 8:30 A.M. when the school day starts. I walk upstairs to the second floor and fill up my water bottle from a machine in an alcove next to the copier. Ms. Kelly, a first grade teacher, and Ms. Lowery, a third grade assistant teacher who is enrolled in the school's alternative certification program, are coming out of one of the student bathrooms with paper towels in their hands. It sounds like they are talking about Ms. Lowery's plans for next year. I walk back down the hallway to Ms. Kelly's room, where she has returned and is starting to prepare for the day.

"We are testing today, Ms. Kerstetter," Ms. Kelly tells me.

"All subjects?" I ask.

"Reading, Part 2," she responds. "They have to read a grade-level text and then a J text." Ms. Kelly says the last phrase about the J-level text with an expression that seems to say "that will be interesting." She is referring to the TerraNova test, a standardized test that she is required to administer annually to assess her students' progress in reading. Per the terms of its charter, City Charter was required to test students once a year and to publicly report the results of the tests, a much less stringent requirement than students and teachers at Oak Grove were subject to. "I have all the kids that don't need accommodations . . . thirty . . . we have quite a few kids with accommodations," Ms. Kelly explains. I clarify that she means that she will have students from both of the first grade classes and she says yes.

About a half hour later, all of the students in Ms. Kelly's class have arrived and are sitting on the carpet for the morning meeting. Ms. Taylor, who identifies as White and female, is participating in the school's alternative certification program and assisting in the two first grade classrooms. She comes into the room with cardboard dividers and places them on a table by the door. "We are out of time for the morning message," Ms. Kelly tells the class. "Nooo," two students with their hands up say. "I think our problem today was the number of people who we had who were talking, and we didn't get as much done because people were talking over each other," Ms. Kelly responds. Ms. Taylor calls a group of students to come with her. Based on what Ms. Kelly said earlier, this would be the group of students who need testing accommodations. The group appears to me to be a mix of girls and boys, and all appear to be students of color.

"Just like yesterday, you are going to sit in a private spot," Ms. Kelly tells the remaining students. "You can whisper talk at your seat until we get booklets," Ms. Kelly says twice. "The booklets will be the last things I pass out before gum or mints." There is a package of Life Savers mints on the table by the door.

Students from Ms. Martinez's first grade class next door arrive. "Think back to where your spot was yesterday," Ms. Kelly says to the students. "Pencil patrol, put one pencil on each table."

Ms. Kelly dismisses the students to get blue dividers. "I should be hearing things like 'excuse me,'" she says as the students attempt to maneuver around each other with the dividers.

Ms. Kelly consolidates the many items that are spread across her teacher table to make room for the students who are sitting there. Three girls sitting at a table by the door debate whether they will choose gum or mints.

"I'm going to change the order," Ms. Kelly says. "I will give gum or mint first." Ms. Kelly stops at the classroom door and talks to Mr. Ramirez, the first grade English Language Learners' (ELL) teacher. "I don't think it's like the [statewide standardized test] where we have to all stay together," she says. Ms. Kelly passes out mints and gum to the students table by table. "I know you all like to tidy but we won't throw away your trash yet," Ms. Kelly explains. Six students are waving their hands in front of their mouths as if they are eating something hot and trying to cool it.

"I read something that said that if you have a mint or chew gum before a test, it helps us think better, so it's good that we have all this powerful stuff," Ms. Kelly shares. I can smell mint from my seat by the cubbies on one side of the room. "Alright, books are coming out now. That means voices are all the way off," Ms. Kelly says. "You can open your books to where your pencils are but don't make any marks."

Ms. Kelly passes out the test booklets to students. "I cannot be more serious than I am right now. No whispering. No talking," she says. Once she has given a test booklet to each student, she says, "Turn to the page, page 12. The question at the bottom of the page is question 23. Read the two sentences and then choose the picture that both sentences tell about."

She reads the same instructions for question 24. I can hear sounds of students chomping on their gum as they answer a few questions in a row. "Take about one more minute. If you're not done, no worries, we have plenty of time," Ms. Kelly says in a friendly, soothing tone. Students at four of the tables seem to be finished, they are sitting back from their tables and looking around. Serena, a small girl who I perceived to be Latina and female, her wavy brown hair pulled back into a ponytail, stretches her arms over her head and looks around her divider at Josie, a girl who I perceived to be White and female and who is sitting across from her. "If you didn't finish, don't worry. You'll have time to finish later on," Ms. Kelly says.

"Turn and put your finger on page 30." Ms. Kelly reads the instructions from a booklet. "Daddy cut a window from a box. Find the word that has the same middle sound as 'cut.' Number 31. Find the word that has the same middle sound as 'make.' Put your finger on number 33 on the next page." Only a few students are putting their fingers on the page. A student who I perceived to be female takes gum out of her mouth, puts it back into her mouth, and holds her pencil over her test booklet. "Uh, uh. Turn your body. You are not talking or looking at any kids. This is the hardest part of the Terra Nova, I think, sitting still and being quiet," Ms. Kelly reminds the class.

"When you are finished question 35, put your pencil in it and close your book. We'll take a short break but not until everyone is done," Ms. Kelly says about a half hour after students have begun the test.

"You may take a four minute break. Walk and talk," Ms. Kelly tells the class a few moments later. The students get up and start walking toward the carpet. "So quiet because they are still testing," Ms. Kelly reminds several students who leave the room for water or the bathroom. She stands in the doorway shushing students in the hallway.

A few minutes later, all of the students have returned to their seats. Ms. Kelly begins to count down from five. "5. Your book is still closed. 4. 3. 2. Your book is still closed. 1. Take a deep breath in and out through your mouth. Zeeero," she says. "I forgot to mention, the gum stays in your mouth.... Open your books again.... Number 35. Turn the page and put your finger next to the blue word 'directions.'"

The room feels less restless now. The students are sitting close to their tables, some putting their fingers on their booklet, looking down at the page as they read the story. Serena taps her feet on the floor several times and then taps her pencil on the table in front of her several times. Three students are sitting back from their tables, looking around the room. "When you have finished number 40, when you have answered all the questions up to number 40, you may put your pencil in your booklet. You may not talk," Ms. Kelly says. I can see at least five students who have closed their booklets.

Ms. Kelly walks around the classroom, looking down at students' test booklets and answers questions. "I'm going to bring around a picture find. If your booklet is closed, you will get one. If you are still working, great! You have plenty of time," she says. Ms. Kelly starts to pass out the picture find worksheets. "The list of things you need to find is at the bottom," she clarifies.

Based on the number of worksheets that Ms. Kelly is passing out, it looks like most students are finished. Ms. Kelly picks up Rosalie's test booklet and points out questions that she did not answer. Ms. Kelly reads the questions to her. Rosalie, a student who I perceived to be Black and female and who I have seen visit Ms. Kelly's room several times to take a nap, begins to move her pencil on the booklet. She looks like she is filling out the answers and then rests her head in her right hand and nods to Ms. Kelly. Ms. Kelly reads the next question to her.

"Thank you so much for giving other kids a chance to finish," Ms. Kelly says to the class and checks the test booklet of another student. It looks like at least two students are still working on the test, including Tanya from Ms. Kelly's class.

Ms. Kelly motions to Rosalie to raise her hand and she does. When Ms. Kelly finishes looking through the other student's booklet, she walks over to Rosalie and looks down at her booklet. "Answer this question and this question," Ms. Kelly says and then walks away. Students are starting to whisper to each other. Ms. Kelly is walking around, collecting students' booklets. "Keep going, Tanya. Keep going," Ms. Kelly says in a quiet voice, putting an index finger over her lips.

About an hour after Ms. Taylor first came in with the dividers, Ms. Kelly picks up the last of the booklets and tells students to get ready for snack.

This observation in Ms. Kelly's first grade classroom was the only time I observed students taking a standardized test across my three months of observing at City Charter. Teachers and administrators at the school appeared to be given much more latitude and autonomy in how they assessed students than were teachers and administrators at Oak Grove Elementary. According to the terms of its charter, City Charter was required to test students once a year, using the same district-wide assessment as traditional public schools for upper elementary school students, and to publicly report the results of the tests. However, the school was exempt from further district-level assessment requirements due to the autonomy granted to charter schools by the school district.

With this autonomy, City Charter was able to implement forms of assessment that were shorter, more integrated into group instruction, and less focused on transmitting test-taking procedures than the assessments required of teachers and students at Oak Grove. Reading assessments at City Charter were completed on an individualized basis and generally took no more than ten to fifteen minutes to complete per student. The ability of teachers at City Charter to frequently assess students on an individualized basis was supported by the small student-to-teacher ratio at the school that allowed lead teachers to meet individually with students while other groups of students worked independently or met with another teacher for small group instruction. This arrangement also allowed students to have much more freedom of movement than they did at Oak Grove Elementary, where students were asked to sit still for hours during standardized tests.

City Charter was also free from much of the school district-level surveillance that teachers and students at Oak Grove were subject to. Part of the lack of surveillance was due to the autonomy that City Charter was given as a charter school and, particularly, an independent charter school that wasn't connected to a charter management organization. Absent frequent and unannounced visits from the school district and the pressures of being labeled a school "in need of improvement," observations at City Charter took on a different tenor.

In the hallway outside Ms. Kelly's classroom I'm greeted by Rachel, a student who I perceived to be Black and female, who is wearing a purple shirt with white polka dots on it today. "Ms. K," she says. "There are two today." I hold the door open for her to enter the classroom and see an adult who appears to me to be White and female with short gray hair sitting in the chair where I usually sit. She is writing in a small notebook that is resting on her lap. I put my belongings in a corner by the classroom's sink and sit back from the carpet a bit toward Ms. Kelly's teacher table.

The woman visiting that day was one of several observers I encountered who were interested in learning more about the school's approach. These observers included teachers who were considering applying to teach at the school, teachers from other schools who were interested in learning more about the school's culture, and parents who were considering whether to enroll their children at City Charter. Additionally, during my first observation in her classroom, Ms. Kelly shared that the school had recently hosted a group from Sweden who were interested in learning about the school's approach to social and emotional learning. The positive tenor and motivations for these observations appeared to create more of a sense of ease in relating to outside observers (including myself) among students and teachers at City Charter.

Part of this sense of ease was related to the school's reputation as an academically successful school. A few years before I observed, the school had been placed in the top tier of all charter schools in the city due to its standardized test scores, a fact that the school advertised prominently on its website. By the time I observed at City Charter, its scores had declined somewhat, but the school still had hundreds of students on a waiting list for admission. Several other charter schools had also been established in and around the neighborhood where City Charter was located, creating more competition for teachers and students. To keep the charter that allowed it to operate, City Charter had to demonstrate in five-year intervals that its students could score well enough on the district's standardized test to avoid being labeled a low-performing school. To attract students and parents to the school, it also had to find a way to differentiate itself from competing charter schools, which the school did with a combined emphasis on academic and social and emotional learning.

In terms of the school's culture and practices, this combined emphasis created an environment that included a culture of urgency focusing on closing achievement gaps, a culture of individual and collective responsibility for student success, and attempts to socialize students into relating in particular ways with teachers and each other through the school's commitment to restorative practices. This chapter examines the ways in which this intersecting set of conditions contributed to structuring teachers' work at City Charter, including their role in creating a set of challenging employment conditions for teachers who worked at the school.

On a warm and windy Thursday afternoon, Ms. Peterson and I are sitting on kid-sized blue plastic chairs outside City Charter School. I have a recorder in my hand, and she has a pile of students' papers on her lap. The school is in the midst of a regularly scheduled fire drill, and we have decided to use the remaining pocket of free time for an interview. We had originally scheduled our interview for Ms. Peterson's planning time but, due to a change in her schedule, we are now squeezing the interview into the twenty minutes Ms. Peterson has during and just after the fire drill, while a classroom assistant monitors her students.

Today Ms. Peterson is wearing a light-gray short-sleeved t-shirt, loose-fitting black pants, an orange and white beaded necklace, and bright orange flat sandals. Her toenails are painted bright orange, and her shoulder-length brown hair is pulled back into a ponytail. Ms. Peterson is in her early thirties and identifies as White and female. At City Charter, she works as a second grade math teacher and also as the school's Math Staff Developer. Ms. Peterson came to teach at City Charter after spending two years teaching at a traditional public school through the Teach For America (TFA) program.

"I actually had no interest in being a teacher at first," she begins and then pauses to revise that statement. "I guess when I was younger, I thought maybe I would be a teacher. And then for a brief moment in college, I thought maybe I would be a teacher, and I tried to major in education. [But] they were like, 'Don't do that if you want to be a teacher.' So, that moment passed and then I majored in Poli Sci [political science], and I wanted to do education policy."

"I thought I would do Teach For America and get two years of experience which is like a wealth of teacher experience," Ms. Peterson continues in an ironic tone. "You know, because most people that do policy have not actually been in the classroom. I deferred Teach For America for a year so that I could do a fellowship at the Department of Education and it was miserable—I hated it so much—and I was like 'Oh, no, well that was my life plan.' And then I did my two years of teaching [with TFA], and I realized if I wanted to do anything to effect change in education, it was not going to be [while] sitting in a cubicle. I mean the entire time, the reason I hated my internship [at the Department of Education] was because the entire time that I was there, I was waiting for a signature for like five months and so the project that I was supposed to work on got delayed five-plus months. I don't know when they started working on it, but not while I was there because I just, all this red tape. Anyway, I thought it was just pointless. So, yeah. I really liked teaching, and it's actually what I want to do."

Elements of Ms. Peterson's narrative were common among her colleagues at City Charter. None of the lead teachers I interviewed at the school had majored in education in college, and all had entered teaching through an alternative certification program. Only one lead teacher, Ms. Washington, had grown up in the same city where City Charter was located. Most teachers I interviewed at City Charter had majored in public policy or political science, and many had education policy-related jobs or internships prior to their first teaching job. One exception was a student teacher, Ms. Taylor, who had changed her major in college from business to education and had completed her student teaching in a public school district in the Midwest. However, even Ms. Taylor decided to pursue an education policy job after graduation rather than go immediately to the classroom and was enrolled in City Charter's alternative certification program.

While teaching was an unexpected profession for many teachers at City Charter, it was also an accessible one—one that could be easily accessed without a teaching degree, due to alternative certification programs, such as TFA and the school's teaching fellowship program, and the ways in which school reform policies such as No Child Left Behind (NCLB) and Race to the Top supported alternative certification. In addition to establishing accountability requirements for schools, NCLB also delineated specific requirements for teachers as part of its Highly Qualified Teacher provision. Highly Qualified Teachers were defined as those with a bachelor's degree, full state certification, and demonstrated subject-matter competence.[1] NCLB allowed "full state certification" to include alternative certification programs, which allowed teachers who were not certified to teach for up to three years while they obtained their certification and permitted states to establish different methods for certification, including passing an assessment in lieu of completing educational coursework.[2]

Teach for America has typically recruited students directly from college campuses, making students aware of alternative teacher certification pathways by employing students as ambassadors to market the program to their peers on campus.[3] The National Center for Education Statistics estimated in school year 2011–2012, nearly 15 percent of teachers in public schools reported that they entered teaching through an alternative certification program.[4]

In the year that I observed at City Charter, the school had been awarded a Race to the Top grant to expand its student teacher training program, which it operated in partnership with another academically successful charter school operator in its district. The funding was designed to support the school in growing its teacher training program from 67 student teachers in 2012 to 415 student teachers by 2016. City Charter and its partner school estimated that they would retain three-quarters of the alternatively certified teachers to teach in their schools, while one-quarter of these student teachers would take jobs in other local charter schools.

Alternative certification programs were first established in the 1980s as a strategy for addressing teacher shortages and have expanded significantly since then. The number of states implementing alternative certification programs grew from eight states in 1983 to forty-three states in 2003.[5] During the

2015–2016 school year, about 18 percent of public school teachers were alternatively certified.[6]

There is some evidence that alternative certification programs have helped to diversify the U.S. teaching workforce. While less than half of students attending public schools in the United States identify as White,[7] the vast majority of teachers in the United States identify as White and female.[8] Studies of the racial and ethnic identities of alternatively and traditionally certified teachers show that alternatively certified teachers are more racially and ethnically diverse than traditionally certified teachers. In school year 2015–2016, 15 percent of alternatively certified teachers identified as Hispanic, compared to 8 percent of traditionally certified teachers, and 13 percent of alternatively certified teachers identified as Black, compared to 5 percent of traditionally certified teachers.[9]

On the other hand, alternative certification programs have facilitated the direction of resources to supporting programs, such as TFA, that have been critiqued for offering at most a short-term "band aid"[10] for teacher shortages and of approaching teaching in economically disadvantaged communities from a deficit mentality[11] and White Savior approach.[12] Founded in 1990 by Wendy Kopp as a senior thesis project, the TFA program recruits college graduates whom the program considers high-achieving to participate in five weeks of intensive teacher training and teach in a school serving economically disadvantaged students for two years. TFA aims for the teachers that it recruits to be able to "capitalize" on their teaching experience by taking what they have learned from teaching in economically disadvantaged communities and using this knowledge to inform their work as leaders in the fields of business, medicine, and public policy, among others.[13] The number of TFA participants has grown from about 500 in the first year of the program's operation in 1990 to over 7,000 twenty years later.[14]

Embedded in the program structure of TFA is the assumption that many, if not most, participants will not remain in teaching for their entire career. Indeed, studies of TFA teacher attrition in both rural and urban placement sites find that TFA teachers are much more likely to leave the profession after three years than teachers not participating in the TFA program.[15] Studies of TFA teachers' effects on student achievement has found mixed results, largely based on which groups of teachers are placed in comparison to TFA teachers: "the predominance of peer-reviewed studies have indicated that, on average, the students of novice TFA teachers perform less well in reading and mathematics assessments than those of fully credentialed beginning teachers. But the differences are small, and the TFA teachers do better if compared with other less-trained and inexperienced teachers."[16]

Of the five lead teachers I observed at City Charter, all entered teaching through alternative certification pathways. Three participated in TFA, one was certified through City Charter's alternative certification program, and one was certified through a program that was not affiliated with the school or TFA. Several of these teachers took a critical perspective on TFA, including teachers who were former members of the program. In my first observation at the school, in Ms. Kelly's first grade classroom, I mentioned to her that one of the aspects of teachers' work that I'm interested in studying is teacher retention. Ms. Kelly, who entered teaching through City Charter's alternative certification program, responded that the school will be an interesting place to study retention because it used to be a place where third-year TFA teachers came to teach for another two years before leaving for graduate school or law school. She said this with an implication that the situation wasn't desirable and that it is changing.

In an interview Ms. Peterson, a former TFA teacher, critiqued the belief that hard work alone can adequately prepare individuals to teach. "Especially in urban education, they tell you you're a genius teacher in TFA after your second year, and you know nothing," she asserted. "I mean like especially in terms of like math instruction, if someone doesn't tell you as a Pre-K teacher to don't say, 'what number comes next,' say 'what is one more than 3,' like you're [laughs] you're, I just think back to like my first year and I'm like, 'I ruined lives'—completely unintentionally—I had the best intention, I worked so hard. I ruined kids' lives! Because they don't, I just didn't have enough support, and no one told me that."

While teachers critiqued TFA for teachers' high turnover rates and the belief that teaching can be done at a high level with minimal preparation, there also were elements of the larger culture of school reform operating at City Charter that seemed less conscious or open to critique. One of these elements was the school's adoption of a sense of urgency around closing achievement gaps. Another was the sense of individual responsibility that Ms. Peterson described when she accused herself of ruining her students' lives. Both of these elements of the school's culture, combined with its lack of employment protections for teachers, contributed to a working environment at City Charter that appeared unsustainable to some teachers.

"The Work Never Really Stops": Teaching to Close Achievement Gaps

Ms. Lowery, a third grade student teacher, and I are sitting around a small table in a pull-out room, where English Language and Special Education teachers meet with students. Ms. Lowery is eating her lunch—a small cheese pizza—while we talk about her experiences working at City Charter for the past three years. Ms. Lowery began working at City Charter as an after-school teacher, then became a student aide, and now works as a student teacher. Ms. Lowery is in her early twenties and identifies as a Black woman. She is finishing her student teaching fellowship this year and is eligible to apply for a position at City Charter next year, but her experiences this year have led her to question whether she wants to continue along that path.

"I started realizing that working in a charter school, you're perpetually trying to narrow the achievement gap, so the work really never stops," she explains. "And I started realizing that people around me, who were not much older than I was, were starting to get burnt out. And disillusioned. And so, it started to worry me."

Ms. Lowery continues, "Like, so and so is 29, 30 years old, and I asked them 'Are you going to teach forever?' And they say, 'I don't know. I don't think I can. I don't think I can sustain this life.' So, that's what started to get me thinking a little bit about it. I started to get worried."

While Ms. Lowery has been working at City Charter for the past three years, this was the first year that as a teaching fellow she experienced many of the demands of being a full-time classroom teacher at the school. "For [City Charter], the school day for a teacher is from 8 to 4. . . . That's not including meetings, planning, or anything. So, I think the hours are definitely tough. I know that the demands of the [school's alternative certification] program have definitely worn me out. The planning and the unit planning. You have to plan an entire unit by yourself from scratch essentially. I mean, based on standards, but essentially, you're taking the standards and crafting your own unit plan and then from there, crafting individual lesson plans for each day. And that gets, that gets to be a lot. . . . It's really tiring, I think, for a lot of teachers to have to plan. . . . And then even during planning time, you really don't have much time because that's when we have meetings. So, there's never really a moment to just breathe."

Studies of school reform implementation have pointed to the use of the language of urgency or crisis among school reformers to justify particular reforms and the speed at which they are implemented.[17] Teachers at City Charter seemed to be embodying this in the number of hours they worked per week and in the individual responsibility they took for their students' academic achievement.

As part of the demographic form I asked teachers to complete at the end of each interview, teachers were asked to indicate approximately how many hours per week they worked on school-related tasks. Ms. Kelly, a first grade teacher at City Charter, reported working about sixty-five hours per week on teaching-related activities. During the interview, she described a typical day: "I get here about 7:30 most days and that is for the prep that I need to have done in the morning, which is [reading] workshop, and so I pull groups, I pull books. I think about what kids need. I try to make copies of anything I need for up until [my] planning block. Often, I'll have a question based on the work I did the night before—which, we'll get to the night time stuff—for someone else in the building, so oftentimes Ms. Matthews, oftentimes Ms. Peterson, oftentimes Ms. Martinez, and I talk to them about those things."

When she describes how she spends her time after school Ms. Kelly mentions what she calls an "apology project"—tutoring students who she taught early in her career out of a belief that she did not teach these students well. "At 4:00, I'm doing—I'm not forced to do this—I'm doing my apology to my classroom two years ago: math tutoring, and that's from 4 until 4:40 or 4:45. It doesn't take a lot of prep or planning because most of what they are doing is really early first grade concept—even kindergarten—conceptual stuff. So, that doesn't take a ton of time. And then I do every night between an hour and two of lesson planning—that's the general lessons for twenty-five kids and about forty minutes of small group planning. Some nights, I won't do that because I will have done it the night before or because I will have done more pieces of it on the weekend. Like, this weekend, I, I'm right now writing the units and the daily plans for math and for science/writing. I did that through tomorrow, so I have some work to do tonight. . . . Most weekends, I do about 8 hours. So . . . that's tough. It's killing me. That's killing me."

While Ms. Kelly spends a lot of time outside her required teaching hours planning lessons, she also spends time each day tutoring students whom she taught previously, what she calls her "apology project." Unlike teachers at Oak Grove Elementary who worked for the school's tutoring program or organized a school reading club for additional pay, Ms. Kelly described offering tutoring without additional pay out of a sense of guilt she feels about her earlier performance as a teacher. "My third year is when—and I think a lot of teachers do this—my third year was when I realized how terribly I had been doing. I looked around and I saw, because I had some perspective and because we had really great professional development and because I had gotten some of those basics not down, but like better, I was able to say things like 'I have not taught these children how to read' or 'Without a plan for writing, writing is not going very well.' So, I felt a lot of responsibility and I also . . . I'm seeing especially things like math, I really messed some stuff up," she says, exhaling a laugh. "Like really . . . After my third year, I didn't think oh I'm terrible at this and I'll get better. Every, my fourth and now my fifth, I have had the same, almost the same feeling just like 'oh, I am so responsible for this, and I'm not doing it well enough yet.'"

The internalization of teachers' personal responsibility for their students' academic progress and the sense of urgency that accompanied this internalization was marked at City Charter.[18] In their efforts to take so much responsibility for their students' learning, teachers seemed to be embodying and reproducing one of the key claims of school reform policies—that the most important factor in a student's academic achievement was whether the student had the opportunity to learn from a highly successful teacher.

Ms. Kelly described her own pathway into the teaching profession using similar terms. "I came to [the city] because that's where my friends were. I was a political science major specializing in Chinese Politics," she explains. "I came, applied for lots of internships. The one I got was at a [school] reform consultancy group. So, like, do you want reform in this or this or this? We'll tell you how to spend your money. Really interesting people in this place. I ended up being the intern for the K through 12 education reform area. And all the research in the world says that the best thing you can do for kids who need a strong education . . . is a good teacher. So, I was like 'yeah, I'll do that.'"

By focusing solely on teachers' contributions to students' educational success, Ms. Kelly and many education reformers were missing or failing to acknowledge the many structural factors, or opportunity gaps, that contribute to educational inequities. As Prudence Carter and Kevin Welner note in *Closing the Opportunity Gap*, the very language of achievement gaps implies a deficit in the achievement of students of color and students from economically disadvantaged households rather than pointing to the structural factors or opportunity gaps that shape educational outcomes.[19] These structural factors include inequities in "health, housing, nutrition, safety, and enriching experiences, in addition to opportunities provided through formal elementary and secondary education," Carter and Welner explain.[20]

Taking so much individual responsibility for students' education also seemed to create the conditions for overwork and burnout that Ms. Kelly pointed to when she acknowledged the amount of work she is doing "is killing me." A consistent theme in my conversations with teachers at City Charter was the relationship between their work and the social mission of education. While most teachers at City Charter did not initially plan to become a teacher, nearly all were attracted to the profession due to the promise of being able to positively influence inequalities in education.

A Culture of Urgency and Individual Responsibility Meets Contingent Labor

In an interview, Ms. Martinez a first grade teacher who identified as Latina and female, compared her experience teaching for two years at a nearby public school with her experience teaching at City Charter. "[In my previous school], I think the administration was sort of scared of central, the teachers were afraid of the administration, and the kids were afraid of the teachers. There were cameras in the school and one of the main things people would . . . say [is] 'should I turn back the camera, would I see it?' That was the main way people used it, so kids thought there were cameras everywhere."

While City Charter did not employ a camera security system to monitor the behavior of its teachers or students, its culture of urgency related to student achievement created an environment in which teachers were expected to be constantly working to improve students' social, emotional, and academic learning. This culture was modeled by the school's principal, who for the three months I observed at the school was serving as the school's principal and teaching fourth grade at the school's upper elementary campus full-time due to the unanticipated departure of a classroom teacher. This was similar to the position that Ms. Matthews assumed when she was tapped to simultaneously co-teach in a second grade classroom, serve as the school's Literacy Coordinator, and teach in a kindergarten classroom half of each day to substitute for a teacher who did not return from maternity leave. Ms. Matthews had retained her Literacy Coordinator position when she transitioned to teaching the kindergarten class in the morning and was now doing much of this work after school because she taught in her second grade classroom in the afternoon.

City Charter's school culture seemed to support and reward this level of work under the banner of a social justice mission. While the school day was structured to give teachers several breaks from their instructional work—two shorter breaks while students were at recess and an hour-long break while students were at specialty classes—teachers usually spent this time engaging in relational work with colleagues to plan lessons or discuss student progress or in relational work with students who needed to engage in a restorative justice process. During one of my observations in a third grade classroom, three teachers who were preparing to leave campus to purchase a cupcake for a colleague's birthday joked that they needed to sneak out of the school since they get "weird looks" from other teachers if they leave the building for lunch.

As salaried employees without union protection, teachers at City Charter usually were not compensated for the extra work they engaged in outside official school hours. According to a veteran teacher I interviewed, teachers' salaries at this school were also $10,000–$30,000 below equivalent positions at local charter and traditional public schools. This information was also supported by an administrator's comment that she had experienced difficulty recruiting teachers over the past year or so because the school's salaries were lower than equivalent positions at other schools. It was not clear why, in a context of ample resources, teachers were not paid more.

Perhaps not surprisingly, when I asked one lead teacher if there was anything that would make it easier to work at her school, she said, "More money. Honestly . . . I say that joking but also, seriously. The amount of time I spend outside of school working is not compensated." One teacher did report asking for and receiving additional pay for additional planning responsibilities she assumed outside school hours but there did not appear to be a formal way that the school managed the accounting of and compensation for additional work performed inside and outside school hours.

In addition to the multiple formal roles that some teachers at City Charter assumed, all teachers at the school played multiple roles in their positions as classroom teachers as they sought to integrate the restorative approaches required of the school's social and emotional learning curriculum with the school's academic curriculum. As a form of gendered labor,[21] and in the case of City Charter as a form of activist labor, relational work has long been marginalized in workplaces.[22] From the earliest efforts to professionalize teaching, credentials such as additional education and higher passing scores on licensure exams have been used to define teacher quality, and relational work has often been devalued when defining the scope of "technical skill and professional knowledge."[23]

As the charter school form of schooling continues to grow, evidence from City Charter suggests that it is important to consider how the flexibility and autonomy granted to charter schools impacts teachers' working conditions. While flexibility and autonomy are often considered positive and valued aspects of teachers' working conditions, in the context of City Charter, they also became part of a culture of overwork. The flexibility of teachers' work schedules, their shifting roles, and the large amount of work that filled teachers' days was a common theme across my observations of teachers' work at City Charter. While teachers at both Oak Grove Elementary and City Charter had plenty of work to do—work that consistently spilled over the boundaries of the official workday—there were several elements of the context of City Charter that made it particularly susceptible to encouraging or promoting overwork among its teachers.

During the time I conducted my research, teachers at City Charter were at-will employees who did not have the same formal bargaining rights as traditional public school teachers in their district. Since this time, teachers at two charter schools in the same city as City Charter successfully won collective bargaining rights at their schools, and two states (Maryland and Hawaii) mandated collective bargaining for all charter school teachers in their state. Nationally, about 11 percent of charter schools were unionized in the United States in school year 2016–2017.[24] The flexibility and autonomy afforded charter schools in terms of designating employees' roles allowed City Charter to recruit its staff into long-term substitute roles, as was the case for Ms. Matthews when she agreed to teach a kindergarten class part-time. In addition, the alignment of the school with the social justice reform mission of school reform policies—to close achievement gaps—also served as a motivation for teachers to engage in long hours of work.

5

"I Would Love to Hear What You Have to Say"

• •

Cultural Reproduction in
Social and Emotional Learning

At the start of the school day, Ms. Lowery sits facing a group of third grade students, who are seated in rows on the carpet in front of her. "I know we did some interesting things over break, and I want you to be able to share," she tells the students. "I'm going to put the clock on for one minute. Partner 1 is going to share and then Partner 2 shares. When I say 'one,' turn to your partner without talking. When I say 'two,' identify Partner 1. When I say 'three,' identify Partner 2. When I say 'four,' Partner 1 starts."

When Ms. Lowery cues them, the students begin sharing what they did over spring break with a student sitting next to them. "I watched TV over break," a student says. "Played games. Arcade games," says another student. "Went to intersession," says a third student. "Partner 2, it's your turn to share what you did over break, starting now," Ms. Lowery says. "I also went to California," a student says. The students are turned toward each other, and many appear to be listening as their partner speaks.

Ms. Lowery asks the students to turn their attention back to her. "I saw a lot of great listening skills from a lot of friends," she says, naming about twelve students. "Just to name a few," she finishes. "I would like to hear what you did over break in one sentence. Over break I . . ." Ms. Lowery says, prompting students to use a complete sentence. "Let's move back to our circle spots in 4, 3, 2, 1."

The students move to sit in a circle shape on the carpet. "Before we begin, how can we show our classmates respect?" Ms. Lowery asks. Several students raise their hands. "Not interrupting," a student says. "Tracking," shares another. "If you have a connection or something to say to them, you can probably [say it to them at recess]," a student adds. "If you cannot show respect, you will not play the game after sharing," Ms. Lowery warns the students. The students begin to share one by one, after raising their hand and being called on by their teacher:

"Went to Charleston."
"Went to the mall and got new shoes."
"Went to the movies."
"Played in a soccer game."
"Watched TV."
"Went to my uncle's house."
"Ate a frog."
"Went to Florida."

"My brother turned two and me and my family celebrated at IHOP," a student who I perceived to be female and Latina says.

Marcus, a student who I perceived to be Black and male, says something so quietly that it is difficult to hear him. It appears that he may be talking about something that happened to a relative or friend. "Is she okay?" Ms. Lowery asks him. "Yes," Marcus answers. "Okay," Ms. Lowery responds. By the end of the morning meeting, about half of the class has described what they did over spring break. Ms. Lowery selects a student who she said was listening particularly well to lead the next activity: a game of Four Corners.

Ms. Lowery, who identifies as a Black woman, is a student teacher at City Charter School, part of the school's alternative teacher certification program. The morning ritual that Ms. Lowery was engaging in with her students was part of City Charter's implementation of the Responsive Classroom approach to education.[1] Responsive Classroom is a privately developed curriculum that helps schools integrate social and emotional learning (SEL) into academic instruction. The key domains of the approach include implementing engaging learning activities that are connected to students' interests, fostering a positive community that encourages students to feel safe taking risks and engaging with peers, and creating an orderly and developmentally appropriate environment that encourages student autonomy.[2]

The morning meetings that teachers facilitated at the beginning of the school day were one example of how the Responsive Classroom approach was integrated into the daily rhythm of life at City Charter. As part of the morning routine in classrooms, teachers provided structured opportunities for students to interact with each other and to share information about their lives outside school. Before engaging in these activities, teachers would often ask students, as Ms. Lowery did, to review the interactional norms of the activity. In doing so, teachers explicitly modeled and reinforced the interactional skills that they hoped students would gain from the activity—making what could be considered a hidden curriculum more visible to students.[3]

In this interactional moment, Ms. Lowery explained to the students that they would be practicing respect, which students appeared to have internalized to mean a form of active listening and turn taking. This skill was also one that students were willing to enforce by attempting to quiet another student while a third student was speaking. Later, during the Four Corners game, Ms. Lowery emphasized what she termed sportsmanship, praising students who handled defeat with grace by calmly walking back to their desks after being called out of the game.

The skills and interactional strategies emphasized by teachers at City Charter as part of the school's commitment to SEL and restorative practices gave students access to skills associated with middle-class norms that could help them engage with educational institutions that adopt these norms with more ease. Across classrooms, there were numerous examples of students practicing autonomy and self-regulation, negotiation and problem-solving, and self-expression. However, across these observations, there were fewer examples of teachers engaging with students' cultures and the nondominant forms of capital they brought to the classroom. Tara J. Yosso describes the dangers of approaching the study and practice of education from a deficit approach:

> In addressing the debate over knowledge within the context of social inequality, Pierre Bourdieu argued that the knowledges of the upper and middle classes are considered capital valuable to a hierarchical society. If one is not born into a family whose knowledge is already deemed valuable, one could then access the knowledges of the middle and upper class and the potential for social mobility through formal schooling. Bourdieu's theoretical insight about how a hierarchical society reproduces itself has often been interpreted as a way to explain why the academic and social outcomes of People of Color are significantly lower than the outcomes of Whites. The assumption follows that People of Color "lack" the social and cultural capital required for social mobility. As a result, schools most often work from this assumption in structuring ways to help "disadvantaged" students whose race and class background has left them lacking necessary knowledge, social skills, abilities and cultural capital (see Valenzuela, 1999).[4]

Rather than organizing schooling around students' perceived deficits, Yosso calls on scholarship and practice to center community cultural wealth, forms of capital that students develop within their families and communities and bring with them to school. These forms of capital include the ability to communicate in more than one language or modality (linguistic capital), knowledge and connection to community history (familial capital), and the skills required to resist and transform inequitable structures (resistant capital), among others. This approach intersects with the discussion of culturally relevant and culturally responsive education in Chapter 3 in that these approaches all value and directly engage the strengths, including the cultural histories and personal narratives, that students bring to the classroom. As this chapter argues, the relative autonomy and flexibility that City Charter had to determine the structure of its school day and the ample resources it was able to mobilize created an environment where students had access to many opportunities to learn and practice interactional skills associated with a White middle-class culture that is dominant in many educational institutions. While this approach can help students navigate similar institutions with more comfort, it also missed the opportunity to transform this culture into one that was more aligned with the wealth of cultural skills that students brought to the classroom.

SEL and Restorative Justice in Schools

Over the past several decades, scholars have begun to examine the role of emotional intelligence (EI) and SEL as predictors of a variety of outcomes, including academic achievement and employment success. The development of the concept of EI grew out of a renewed focus on the idea that individuals possess multiple intelligences[5] beyond the cognitive capacities measured by IQ tests. EI can be defined as "the ability to carry out accurate reasoning about emotions and the ability to use emotions and emotional knowledge to enhance thought."[6] EI includes individuals' abilities to perceive others' emotions and to identify their own emotions; to use emotions to aid cognitive activities such as problem-solving; to understand the discourse of emotion, including the relationships between emotions; and the ability to manage their own and others' emotions.[7] Among scholars, the development of EI as a concept is generally attributed to Salovey and Mayer's efforts to outline a framework for the study of EI as an intelligence, distinct from social or cognitive intelligence.[8]

The concept of EI became popularized in the public realm with the publication of Daniel Goleman's *New York Times* bestselling book *Emotional Intelligence*.[9] The popularization of the concept has contributed to a proliferation of research on EI, mainly among psychologists, that has sought to refine and test the concept of EI and to examine its ability to predict outcomes in education, employment, personal relationships, and health. A meta-analysis of research related to EI found that EI predicts positive social outcomes for both adults and children.[10] Children with higher levels of EI (as assessed by peers, parents, or teachers) are significantly more likely to experience better social relations and to have higher levels of social competence.[11]

In the years following the publication of *Emotional Intelligence*, politicians and educators began experimenting with ways to promote EI in schools. In the United States, "[b]y 1997, at least 22 formal programs of socioemotional learning had been tested in one or more schools or school systems, with some programs emphasizing emotional intelligence throughout the school's entire curriculum."[12] In Illinois, learning standards associated with SEL were created for each grade level from kindergarten through twelfth grade, spanning the skills of identifying emotions, empathizing with others, and resolving conflicts nonviolently.[13] The incorporation of SEL and EI into school curricula has extended beyond the United States to Asia, Europe, Australia and New Zealand, Africa, and Latin America.[14]

At City Charter, SEL was institutionalized in the school through the implementation of the Responsive Classroom curriculum, the adoption of a restorative justice approach to school discipline, and the employment of a full-time Social and Restorative Justice Coordinator. As described at the beginning of this chapter, the Responsive Classroom approach at City Charter involved teachers setting aside dedicated time for students to learn and practice an interactional skill such as respect or teamwork. This time often involved students practicing communicating with peers and adults, one-on-one and in a larger group. The interactional skills that students practiced during their morning meetings with teachers were also reinforced throughout the school day as part of academic activities.

In addition to implementing the Responsive Classroom approach, City Charter also modeled its disciplinary policies on principles of restorative justice. Restorative justice approaches have been promoted as an alternative to zero-tolerance and other exclusionary discipline policies that disproportionately punish students of color, especially Black students.[15] Restorative justice practices were originally developed within the criminal justice system as an alternative to the traditional sentencing system.[16] Restorative justice approaches emphasize communication or mediation between victims and offenders; offenders are encouraged to take responsibility for their actions and to take action toward repairing the harm they have caused.[17] Beginning in Australia in 1994, schools have experimented with adopting restorative justice practices as alternatives to traditional disciplinary systems.[18]

Restorative justice was originally envisioned and implemented as a formal conference between victims and offenders. As this process has been implemented in schools, restorative justice has come to include a set of formal and informal strategies that can be characterized as reactive (e.g., formal conferencing, peer mediation, and informal classroom or hallway conversations following an offense) or proactive (e.g., the adoption of curricula that focus specifically on SEL).[19] Research has found that "positive, proactive disciplinary measures" are associated with a lower use of school suspensions as a disciplinary strategy.[20] However, racial inequalities in discipline continue to be reproduced in restorative practices that are created as alternatives to the zero-tolerance model.[21] Assessments of one such restorative practice, Schoolwide Positive Behavior Support Implementation, found that White and Latino students were less likely to be at risk of behavioral failure (measured by frequency of office discipline referrals) than were Black students.[22] The same study also found that Black students were disproportionately selected by school staff members to engage in restorative practices.

SEL and restorative approaches to discipline were the dominant culture of education at City Charter School and were practiced across classrooms. As this chapter will demonstrate, explicit instruction in emotional awareness and interactional skills at City Charter provided the opportunity for students to gain access to skills and norms associated with a White middle-class culture that is dominant in many educational institutions. At the same time, the lack of engagement of students' families, communities, and cultures as part of the disciplinary culture and SEL curriculum at the school, meant that nondominant cultural capital—the cultural strengths and assets that students of color brought to school—were marginalized in classrooms that adopted dominant cultural practices.

"I Would Love to Hear What You Have to Say": Self-Expression and Shared Control

In a third grade classroom, students are gathered on the carpet in front of the student teacher, Ms. Lowery, for their morning meeting. "Good morning," Ms. Lowery says to the students. "Good morning, Ms. Lowery. How are you doing today?" the students say in unison.

"I am doing okay. I woke up really early and thought we could be having a delay," Ms. Lowery replies, referring to the inch of snow outside. "I like how friends are doing their silent 'yes' and 'me, too' signs. But I am excited that we will be doing science first today."

Ms. Lowery tells the students that since there aren't many students in the classroom yet, they can pick which greeting they would like to do this morning. The students vote and select a game called "My Momma Told Me." The students stand in a circle, and Ms. Lowery asks the students to think of their movement and to remind her of the rules for the movements. "No falling on the carpet," a student says. "Safe moves," another adds.

Ms. Lowery begins the game by chanting, "My momma told me to do my name just like I do" and then says her name, "Ms. Lowery," as she shakes her hands above her head. The students all repeat her name and her movement, saying "Ms. Lowery" as they wave their hands above their heads. The greeting game continues, with each student taking a turn to add their name and a movement and the students repeating each name and movement. There are smiles and laughter as the game travels around the circle of students.

Morning meetings at City Charter were one of the settings in which teachers sought to integrate SEL into the school day. During morning meetings like the one Ms. Lowery facilitated, some teachers ceded aspects of control over the classroom to students, allowing students to vote on which game they would play as a class or allowing a single student to direct an activity. In one first grade classroom, the teacher selected a student at random each week to bring in three items that were important to the student to share with the class. During these times, the teacher would sometimes take the role of a student, sitting in the circle of students and raising her hand to be called on by the student who was sharing that day. By setting aside time for students to share about their lives outside school, City Charter teachers communicated their interest in students as individuals and their belief that the classroom could be a space where students were able to express this individuality. In doing so, students were invited to cultivate a sense of ease in communicating with adults and other students, a cultural practice that has been associated with the concerted cultivation approach of middle-class families.[23]

Throughout the school day, teachers provided similar opportunities for students to communicate with peers and teachers about academic content. In a first grade classroom, Ms. Martinez pauses after reading several pages of a book aloud to students. "What do you know about this character so far?" Ms. Martinez asks the students. Ms. Martinez, who identifies as Latina and female, leans toward the students and in a low, excited tone says, "Turn and tell your partner." She crouches on the carpet and listens to a student sharing with his partner. "Back to me in 3, 2, 1," she says and returns to a chair at the front of the carpet. "What do we know about Poppleton?" Ms. Martinez asks, referring to the main character in the book.

Sheila, a student who I perceived to be Black and female, raises her hand. "I know we are thinking and then we will raise a quiet hand," Ms. Martinez says to the rest of the class before calling on Sheila. "He was a city pig," Sheila responds. Ms. Martinez repeats what Sheila has said and then continues reading the book. This process was repeated frequently throughout classrooms in City Charter during reading, writing, math, and science/social studies lessons. In the midst of lessons, students were given the opportunity to discuss what they were thinking with a partner and to share their thoughts with their teacher and fellow classmates. These interactive moments provided an opportunity for students to practice sharing their opinions and ideas with others, a key skill that has been identified as part of the dominant culture at many post-secondary institutions.[24]

Due to the flexibility afforded to charter schools—in terms of the lower burden of surveillance and standardized testing than teachers at Oak Grove encountered, the ability to extend the school day and school year, and to hire additional staff members for each classroom—teachers at City Charter had more time and other resources in which to implement SEL and restorative approaches. As Ms. Lowery describes, "For instance, I just had a heart to heart with one of the students today where she broke down crying because she felt bad about being a bully. It took an hour and fifteen [minutes] out of her reading time to do that. Some schools would not be okay with that. I think over here, it's like it's necessary, it needs to be done, so we're going to take this time to do this. Because otherwise, they'll never be able to access the material because they have other issues." The resources that City Charter was able to mobilize to have two to three staff members in a classroom at most times and the ability to extend its school day and school year made it possible and "okay" to spend extended periods of time on SEL and cultivating students' repertoires in sharing their opinions and ideas and speaking comfortably with peers and adults.

"Is that a Smart Spot?": Autonomy and Self-Regulation

One afternoon in a second grade classroom, one of the two co-lead teachers, Ms. Matthews, dismisses the students from the carpet for their independent writing time. "Find a smart spot," Ms. Matthews encourages the students. The students begin to leave the carpet and move toward one of the classroom's five tables, taking a composition notebook and a pencil from one of the red bins in the center of each table. From there, the students spread out across the classroom. Three students sprawl on the carpet where the students were just seated; one takes up residence on the carpet beside a cozy red sofa. Other students find a spot at one of the classroom's five tables. "Look how focused Amy is on her work. Joseph, I'm not sure that is going to help you write a poem. Guys, let's make sure we are making smart choices," Ms. Matthews urges the students. Ms. Matthews identifies as White and female and has been teaching at City Charter for four years. She walks around the classroom for a few minutes, encouraging students to begin writing their poems, before sitting at the table in the back of the classroom and helping a student brainstorm ideas for the composition.

"He says he can be rude if he wants to!" Kevin, a student who I perceived to be male and Latino, exclaims in a frustrated tone. Ms. Hamilton, the classroom's paraprofessional, stops by the table to talk with Kevin and the student he is referring to, Darren, and then facilitates an apology between the two students. A student sitting at the head of the table, who I perceive to be female, leaves to work on the carpet near the sofa where I am sitting. She joins another student, and they work independently and quietly about two feet from each other.

A few minutes later, nearly all of the students are writing in their notebooks, with the exception of one student, whom I perceive to be male, who is playing on the carpet at the front of the room. "You need to come work at a table," Ms. Hamilton says, directing the student to one of the tables with an empty seat. He follows her and takes a seat at a table. "Are you using kind words here? If not, let me know. I can help," Ms. Hamilton says to the students at the table where Kevin is sitting. Ms. Matthews hands a pair of noise-canceling earphones to a student at the same table who seems distracted. The student puts the headphones on for a few seconds and then takes them off again.

At the end of the writing lesson, the students are back on the carpet, listening as Ms. Matthews reads a poem. Kayla, a student whom I perceived to be Black and female, moves from her spot to a different part of the carpet, and Ms. Matthews gives her a quiet thumbs up as she continues discussing the poem with the students. As the students begin to leave the carpet, Ms. Matthews turns to the student who moved. "Kayla, can I give you a compliment? You saw you weren't solving the problem quietly, so you moved away," she says, giving Kayla a high five.

In each of the classrooms at City Charter, there were times during the school day when students could choose where they would complete assignments, usually during independent reading or writing time. Students were given the autonomy to choose where they would do their work within the limits of choosing a "smart spot"—usually defined by teachers as a space where students would be unlikely to be distracted or to distract others. The classroom spaces in City Charter were designed so that these choices would be meaningful—students could choose between one or two carpet spaces, any of the tables, and sometimes a beanbag chair or sofa as well. Students were explicitly taught and held accountable for choosing a spot that would not interfere with their ability to complete their work. Students had the freedom to move to a better spot, as the girl at the table did, if their initial spot did not work out and to try different techniques for focusing, as Ms. Matthews invited a student to do when she offered him the noise-canceling headphones.

Students were also granted a measure of autonomy in how they completed their math assignments. Students' independent work assignments were structured on a weekly basis where activities were characterized either as a "must do" or a "may do." Students were required to complete all of their "must do" assignments in a given week before they were allowed to participate in instructional games that were classified as "may do" assignments. Teachers checked students' folders weekly to assess whether they had completed all of their assignments, and students could be prohibited from participating in "may do" activities for a week if they had not completed their "must do" assignments by the due date.

By allowing students a degree of autonomy in where and when they would complete their independent work assignments, teachers were beginning to prepare students for skills that researchers have associated with success in postsecondary institutions. The repertoires required to successfully enact the role of college student are different in many respects than those required of primary and secondary students.[25] They include the ability to work independently, to wait longer for feedback on a particular task, and to prioritize educational tasks in a context of less structure and fewer competing priorities.[26] In teaching and enforcing the skills required to select a "smart spot" and manage work independently, teachers were emphasizing the practices of self-regulation and self-awareness. Self-awareness, defined as "an individual's ability to critically examine and reflect upon personal strengths and weaknesses in order to develop a plan for addressing self-diagnosed deficits as a means to successfully enact the role" was found to be a key capability needed to successfully transition to the college student role.[27]

Teachers at City Charter were aided in teaching these skills by the structure and autonomy of their school. Without the requirement to implement numerous and lengthy standardized tests, students could engage with more autonomy in academic assignments and had more time to do so. Students were also granted permission to move more freely about their classrooms more frequently than they might in a context with more standardized testing and surveillance.

"What Can I Do to Make You Feel Better?": Negotiation and Problem-Solving

One afternoon in Ms. Kelly's classroom, the first grade students are watching a video as they finish their lunch. Michael, a second grader whom I perceived to be White and male, enters the room and shows a paper he is holding to Ms. Kelly. After the video ends, Ms. Kelly asks Michael if he would like to talk to a few students or the whole class. Michael opts to speak to the whole class.

Ms. Kelly motions for him to walk to the center of the carpet and tells him to speak up. Michael reads from his paper. It is an apology for calling members of the first grade class "losers" at the school's Fast Math Competition last Friday. After Michael finishes reading his apology, Ms. Kelly tells the students that they have time for two questions. A student whom I perceived to be female raises her hand, and Ms. Kelly acknowledges her. "I don't know what you said [at the competition], but I accept your apology," she says. Another student, whom I also perceive to be female, raises her hand, and Ms. Kelly acknowledges her. "I wasn't there on Friday, but even if we lost, I'm glad the second graders won," she shares.

"Thanks, Michael, that's great. I think a lot of the kids feel better," Ms. Kelly concludes, and Michael leaves the classroom.

This ritual, while more public than most, was repeated often throughout the school day at City Charter. When conflicts emerged among students or between students and teachers, teachers sought to transmit repertoires related to negotiation, boundary-setting, and conflict resolution. Students were encouraged to talk to each other about their needs, to imagine how another student might feel in a given situation, and to act in ways that would repair harm when it had been committed.

Several weeks after the apology described above, Ms. Kelly talks with Bryan, who has returned to the classroom from recess before the other students. "Ms. Kelly, Amanda told everyone I kissed her three times but I didn't," Bryan says, sounding frustrated. "It sounds like you didn't like that," Ms. Kelly responds. "No," Bryan confirms. "Well, what are you going to tell her?" Ms. Kelly asks as she helps Bryan hang up his jacket. "That I don't want her to do that anymore, please," Bryan responds. Ms. Kelly laughs. "Ooh, I like that please. I'm sure that will convince her," she says. A few minutes later, Amanda walks into the classroom and comes over to Bryan. "Bryan, I'm sorry," Amanda says. Kelsey, who says she started the rumor, also comes over to Bryan and apologizes. Ms. Kelly facilitates parts of the interaction, motioning for Kelsey to stop spinning on one foot while she apologizes and encouraging Bryan to listen to Kelsey and Amanda.

Rather than using her authority to follow up with the girls herself or minimizing what Bryan had experienced, Ms. Kelly empathizes with what she imagines Bryan might be feeling and then asks him what he could do to solve the problem that he identified. In doing so, she is modeling how she would like Bryan to resolve the conflict and leaving room for him to choose his response. When informed about a conflict between or among students, teachers at City Charter often responded by asking the offended party what they planned to do, reminding students that they had choices about how they could respond. Alongside this open-ended question, teachers explicitly taught students how to ask for what they needed and facilitated apologies between students so that students had an available script that they could call upon when their teacher asked them what they were going to do.

In some cases, students had internalized these cultural repertoires[28] and were able to enact them with minimal teacher intervention, as did the girls in Ms. Kelly's first grade classroom when they engaged Bryan at the beginning of class rather than waiting for him to tell them he did not appreciate their behavior. In other cases, teachers were more actively involved in facilitating the restorative process, particularly for more significant offenses, such as physical harm or destruction of property. Larger-level offenses involved the ritual of repairing harm to a student or teacher who had been offended, as shown in this example from a second grade classroom.

"Joseph, you need to come to my table," Ms. Matthews, a second grade lead teacher says to a student. "Do you know why I am asking this?" Ms. Matthews describes an incident that happened the day before in which one student placed another student's coat in the boys' bathroom and a third student put the coat in a toilet.

Joseph, a student who I perceive to be Latino and male, is joined by Darren, a student who I perceived to be Black and male. "What can you do nice for Jacob to show him you are sorry?" Ms. Matthews asks the two boys sitting in front of her. One of the students responds very quietly. "We might have to talk to your mom about that but is there something we can do now, like draw him a picture?" Ms. Matthews asks. One of the students mentions that Jacob likes battleships, and they decide that they could draw him a battleship picture.

"What are you going to do for me?" Ms. Matthews asks. "I had to touch a coat in the toilet." Joseph and Darren are silent. "Think about that," Ms. Matthews urges them. "Both of you also lied the first time I asked you, so I need to feel like I can trust you again."

"I won't do it again," Joseph says. "Well, of course you won't do it again," Ms. Matthews says as if that is obvious. "If you are going to do something nice for Kevin, what are you going to do for me?" "Miss recess," suggests Darren. "Well, yes, you are definitely going to miss recess," Ms. Matthews says. She describes how it felt to pick a coat out of the toilet and to get toilet water on her hands and suggests that there might be something the boys could do that is related to cleaning up.

"We can help clean up [the classroom]," Joseph offers. Ms. Matthews agrees that the classroom could use a cleaning. "And you are cleaning up something that isn't your mess, so why don't you start on that," she says. Darren and Joseph start to clean up the classroom. Darren sweeps the floor with a small dustpan and brush. "This is looking better guys, thank you. I'm starting to feel a little bit better," Ms. Matthews says.

The work of repairing harm provided an opportunity for students to engage in a dialog with peers and/or those in authority. This was often a time-consuming process and required teachers to set aside time during students' recess periods to engage in this work. Teachers at City Charter used the process of repairing harm as an alternative to issuing detentions or suspensions to students. When students repeatedly distracted other students or threatened physical harm, teachers also asked students to "take a break" away from the other students for thirty seconds to several minutes or called on the school's Restorative Justice Coordinator to remove students from class for individual conferencing.

Cultural Reproduction at City Charter School

City Charter requires its teachers to adopt approaches to organizing their classrooms drawn from restorative justice and Responsive Classroom methods that focus on a relational, rather than punitive, approach to behavior management. Teachers enacted a common set of practices oriented to increasing students' noncognitive skills, including a facility and ease in speaking to adults and peers, an ability to self-regulate and manage work independently that goes beyond the following of a routine and delineated set of tasks, and an ability to negotiate and solve conflicts peacefully. These skills and interactional strategies closely align with the evaluative standards of middle-class institutions and, as a result, potentially prepare students to engage with educational institutions that adopt this dominant culture with more ease. However, missing from this approach was an engagement with students' cultures and the nondominant forms of capital they brought to the classroom. While teachers provided opportunities for students to share information about their weekend or to bring in an object to share with other students in the class as part of morning meeting, a reciprocal exchange of learning seemed missing from these interactions. Providing more opportunities for students to share about their families and communities, to connect what they are learning to their own personal and community history, and to teach skills that they have learned outside the classroom to adults and peers could have made cultural learning at City Charter travel both ways, from teacher to student and from student to teacher.

Conclusion

• •

Near the end of my interview with Ms. Peterson, a second grade teacher at City Charter School, I ask her about the work that she does to help students with challenges they face outside school. "I think something our school has tried to really be proactive about is . . . trying to understand that extreme poverty is actually like a form of trauma and so the way that you approach kids and the way that you approach struggles that they're having in school perhaps is . . . in many cases like the way that you would approach someone who had suffered extreme forms of trauma. But at the same time, we know there shouldn't be lowered expectations in terms of academics and the same with behavior," she says. "And so, there's a ton of supports that get put in place in terms of like special spots and special plans and talking to parents. And making sure that, even though it drives me crazy that I think there should be a cutoff at some point for breakfast and you get a breakfast bar, you can't not feed a kid, that's really important. Like Jennifer's family needs the school to provide food for her. But you also need to be on the carpet for the mini lesson, you can't miss that. So, I think it's sort of like not only individual teachers but the school as a whole is always trying to struggle between what we know kids need, what we are actually able to provide, and the balance between."

This book has explored the balancing act that schools and their teachers do to respond to students' social, emotional, and material needs and the contextual factors that influence schools' abilities to meet students' needs. It has done this from the perspective of teachers' work at two elementary schools, Oak Grove Elementary and City Charter School. The teachers at both of these schools, as well as teachers across the United States, experience moments throughout the school day when they are met by a student who is hungry after missing breakfast, tired after waking up to greet a parent who has just come home from working a double shift, or stressed from sharing a small living space with many family members. These needs stem from long-standing inequities in education, employment, and housing and are racially patterned.

Meeting students' basic needs is an important prerequisite to ensuring that students are prepared to succeed academically. This book has detailed the many ways in which teachers work to meet students' social, emotional, and material needs as part of their daily work in schools. This labor includes providing food for students' breakfast, lunch, or snack to fill in gaps between what students need and what schools and families are able to provide. It includes providing a place for students to sleep when they are ill or tired. Teachers' labor also includes the work of cultivating students' belonging and connection to school by developing rapport with individual students, providing opportunities for students to connect their lived experiences to the academic curriculum, and helping students navigate relationships with peers and adults.

As teachers engage in this work, there are contextual factors that constrain and enable teachers' and schools' abilities to meet students' needs. These include school funding levels, the effects of school reform policies, and school-level practices. These contextual factors are multidimensional and interconnected. For example, the multidimensional effects of school reform policies include the level of autonomy granted to charter schools versus traditional public schools and the symbolic status that schools gain from being labeled "low-performing" or "high-performing." School reform policies connect to levels of school funding by providing schools with the symbolic capital of being able to label themselves "high-performing" and allowing schools aligned with particular school reform networks to mobilize funding from private foundations aligned with the movement, as City Charter did.

This book has also sought to illuminate how these contextual factors shaped different conditions of learning at Oak Grove and City Charter. The experiences of teachers at Oak Grove help us to see the way that the audit culture of school reform requires teachers to constantly be engaged in producing evidence of student learning and the ways in which school reform policies have created an additional form of surveillance for both teachers and students. The heavy emphasis on testing at the school created conditions of learning that are associated with reproducing the skills and knowledge associated with working-class jobs, including following directions and deferring to authority. These were not the only types of interactional skills being taught at Oak Grove, as the example from a "normal" day in Ms. Jackson's class demonstrated, showing that even in the context of external surveillance and the audit culture of school reform policies, teachers were working to open up space for students to have greater voice and engagement in academic learning.

At City Charter, the autonomy the school enjoyed as an independent charter school and the resources it was able to mobilize allowed the school to pursue a path where academic learning and social and emotional curricula were
interwoven throughout the school day. The types of restorative practices that
the school implemented as part of its social and emotional learning allowed students to be taught explicitly and to practice skills associated with middle-class
employment and interactional styles, including negotiating with those in
authority and communicating with adults and peers with greater ease. The
drawback of making these practices the dominant culture of the school was that
City Charter engaged in its own process of social reproduction in which White
middle-class interactional styles were elevated above the other forms of cultural
capital that students, especially students of color and students from economically disadvantaged families, brought with them to school.

The experiences of teachers in City Charter and Oak Grove Elementary
point to some of the ways in which schools and their teachers are constrained
by, implicated in, and are working to resist the reproduction of social inequalities. Both City Charter and Oak Grove were situated within communities with
historical and ongoing inequities related to housing and homeownership. For
residents who lived in Oak Grove, the desegregation of the community was
accompanied by an increase in affordable housing; however, this housing
was limited to affordable housing rental properties, which limited the wealth-
building prospects for individual families and the ability of the school district
to derive additional revenue from property taxes. This decision contributed to
the creation of Oak Grove as a "low-income school," which welcomed students
from the affordable housing surrounding the school, while at the same time
contributed to limiting the resources that were available for serving students.
For the families who lived in the neighborhoods surrounding City Charter,
city-sponsored economic development led to rising property values and property taxes that were difficult to afford, leading many Black working-class
families to move away from the neighborhood and White middle-class families
to move into the neighborhood. While City Charter drew its student population
from across the city, it also served as an attractive option for new White middle-
class residents living in the neighborhoods surrounding the school. The more
affluent families that City Charter was able to attract helped the school
raise the funds needed to open new facilities, operate on a year-round extended
day basis, and hire the staff needed to implement its intensive social and emotional learning curricula, although these staff appeared to be underpaid compared to traditional public school teachers in the same district.

Inequities in students' and their families' access to food, health care, and
housing shaped the types of student needs that teachers in both schools in this
study responded to. Addressing the policies and practices that contribute to
reproducing these inequities is an important place to start if we want to make

sure that students have access to the basic resources that equip them to engage in academic learning. Addressing social inequities at the upstream or more structural level can help to take pressure off schools to provide for students' material needs. Rather than offering a set of prescriptions, I would encourage policymakers and community planners to engage residents meaningfully in discussions about economic development, employment, education, and income supports, especially residents who have been historically marginalized from such discussions.

At the school level, school district officials, administrators, and teachers all play a role in the types of environments and learning opportunities that students encounter in schools, including whether these perpetuate processes of social reproduction and whether they recognize and engage the strengths and assets students bring with them to school. School reform policies can mediate how difficult or how easy it is for schools to create environments that honor and engage students' lived experiences and create room for different interactional styles and processes of learning. Rather than reducing the process of education to performance on standardized tests, school reform policies should help to create the conditions of learning that would allow students of differing racial, ethnic, and economic backgrounds to thrive in school. In helping to create these conditions of learning, policymakers and administrators should actively involve students, parents, and teachers in discussions about educational policies and practices, ensuring that the voices of those most directly affected by policy decisions have an active role in shaping those decisions.

Appendix

• •

To better understand how schools are organized to meet the nonacademic needs of their students and how school reform policies influence the daily lived experiences of teachers and students in public elementary schools, I drew on methods of inquiry associated with institutional ethnography, first articulated by Dorothy Smith.[1] Institutional ethnography provides a way to produce knowledge about the social organization of inequalities without abstracting them from the daily lived experiences of the people who are affected by them. It begins from the actual experiences of people, building an account of their daily activities, and then moves beyond the local to map the extra-local social relations embedded in policies, practices, and institutions that help to structure individuals' daily lives. In this study, institutional ethnography is employed to document the actions that teachers engage in to meet the social, emotional, and material needs of their students; to analyze how extra-local factors, such as school organization and school reform policies, enable and constrain this work; and to assess how these extra-local factors may influence the types of noncognitive skills that are transmitted to students. In the sections that follow, I describe the data collection and analysis methods that I used as part of this broader methodological approach.

Gaining Access to Schools

The process of gaining access to my field sites, City Charter and Oak Grove Elementary (both pseudonyms), contrasted greatly between the two school sites. This process also reflected many of the themes related to autonomy, bureaucracy, and rationalization in traditional public versus public charter schools that I discussed in the introduction. For both schools, the process of gaining access initially came from a personal connection after I struggled to gain access to schools through more formal means. In the case of City Charter, access began with a meeting with a friend of a friend, a woman who was currently teaching at a traditional public school and her mentee, who was a student teacher at City Charter School. The three of us met to discuss my project and, at the end of the meeting, the student teacher suggested that I contact one of her school's administrators to request permission to conduct my research at the school. An email to the school administrator resulted in an in-person meeting at City Charter School, during which I discussed my project and eventually received permission to conduct research at the school, pending the completion of a background check. After completing my background check and meeting with the school's Human Resources Manager, I was approved to conduct research at the school.

My experience attempting to recruit my second school, a traditional public school, proceeded much less smoothly. Each of the traditional public school districts in the region where I was conducting my research had established their own Institutional Review Board (IRB) process, which meant that I would need the permission of the school system's central office before I would be permitted to conduct research within their school system. I first met with an individual who was in charge of the IRB process in the same school district as City Charter School, hoping to gain access to a traditional public school within the same district. Unfortunately, the official informed me that the school system had several ongoing studies currently being implemented in their school district and were not currently approving new proposals. He encouraged me not to spend the time completing the lengthy paperwork required to submit an application to the school district.

I then turned my attention to the school districts immediately surrounding City Charter's school district. I engaged in a variety of strategies in my efforts to gain school district IRB approval: I reached out to teachers and administrators at individual schools and used their support in an attempt to bolster my application, I met with the former Human Resources Director of one of the school districts and asked her for feedback on my application, and I secured permission to use the name of someone who worked closely with another school district in an attempt to bolster my application with a third district. None of these strategies yielded an approval of my IRB application.

In the end, my proposal was accepted by the last school district that I applied to that was still adjacent to City Charter's school district. In this case, I reached out to a friend of a friend from college who taught in this school district, and she agreed to connect me with her administrator. After receiving permission from the administrator to move forward with my application, I submitted my fourth proposal to a school district IRB and gained approval, with minor revisions requested, to conduct research in the school district. The school district did not require a background check but did require that I submit a form with the principal's signature, indicating her support of the project. My friend invited me to meet her after school, where she helped me to recruit other teachers and to obtain the principal's signature on the permission form.

The School Sites

City Charter School is a public charter school located in a medium-sized city in the Mid-Atlantic region of the United States. The school was founded in 2004 as a PreK-grade two school and has since expanded to offer a PreK-twelfth grade program on two campuses. During the school year in which I observed, the school served 950 students in grades Pre-K through ten and was in the process of expanding to serve students in eleventh and twelfth grades. Students gain admittance to City Charter by participating in an annual lottery, and the school regularly maintains a wait-list of students whose families are hoping to gain access to the school. City Charter is classified as a Title I school (with at least 40 percent of students living below the federal poverty line), and a majority of its students qualify for free and reduced meals. During the year that I observed in the school, 60 percent of City Charter's students were eligible for free and reduced meals, 43 percent of the students identified as Black/African American , and 32 percent of students identified as Latino/Hispanic.

As a public charter school, City Charter has the freedom to determine its own daily and yearly school schedule. City Charter operates on an extended-day and year-round schedule and offers programs before and after school and during the school's intersession breaks free of charge to students who qualify for free and reduced meals. The school estimates that by participating in this programming and in the school's year-round schedule, students gain an additional 1,000 hours of instruction over and above students attending a traditional public school.

City Charter also operates its own teacher training and certification program in partnership with another local charter school and selects many of its teachers from the pool of those who complete the program. On its website, City Charter prominently displays the standardized test scores of its students. In the year before I observed at the school, more than three-quarters of City Charter's students had scored at proficient or advanced levels in math and nearly three-quarters had scored at the same levels in reading. These scores were twenty percentage points higher than the average standardized testing scores of the city's other public charter schools.

The second school in this study, Oak Grove Elementary, is a traditional public school located in a suburban neighborhood about nine miles from City Charter's elementary school campus. Oak Grove Elementary was built in the 1960s as a neighborhood school and continues to draw its student population primarily from the apartment complexes that surround its campus. The school also has a special education emphasis and draws students needing special services from across its school district. Oak Grove Elementary serves a much larger population of elementary school students than does City Charter. According to the school's website there were approximately 760 students enrolled in kindergarten through grade five at Oak Grove Elementary during the year in which I observed. Oak Grove Elementary was also classified as a Title I school and, according to data from the state department of education, 88 percent of students attending Oak Grove Elementary were eligible for free and reduced meals. At the time of my research, the vast majority of students at Oak Grove Elementary (95 percent) identified as Black/African American or Latino/Hispanic.

As a traditional public school, Oak Grove Elementary operates on the nine-month schedule traditionally associated with public schools in the United States and provides 180 days of required instruction as mandated by its state education agency. With permission from a No Child Left Behind waiver from the federal government, Oak Grove Elementary's state education agency measured all schools' progress by an index that takes into account students' standardized testing scores, the size of achievement gaps between subgroups of students, and the growth schools have made in closing achievement gaps. During the year that I observed, Oak Grove Elementary was classified in the second to last tier of schools in its state because it had not met any of its achievement targets that year, according to data published on the state education agency's website.

Data Collection

The fieldwork for this study, which includes classroom observations and interviews, focused on the experiences of elementary school teachers working at City Charter and Oak Grove Elementary. From March 2013 to April 2014, I conducted 245 hours of classroom observations and 19 interviews in the two schools. I spent between two and three months at each school, conducting observations and interviews at City Charter from March through May 2013 and at Oak Grove Elementary from December 2013 through February 2014. At City Charter, an administrator helped me recruit teachers to participate in my study by sending an email to all teachers in the school, inviting them to participate. At Oak Grove Elementary, a teacher at the school who I knew through a friend, connected me with her principal and accompanied me on recruitment visits to teachers' classrooms one day after school.

Classroom Observations

In each of the schools, I completed half- and full-day observations of teachers' work in their classrooms, visiting teachers' classrooms multiple times over the course of the observation period. During these observations, I documented teachers' daily activities in their classrooms, paying particular attention to teachers' attempts to meet students' social, emotional, or material needs. These daily activities included whole class instruction, meetings with small groups of students, supervision of students' breakfast and lunch time, and meetings with colleagues. I also observed informal interactions between teachers and parents (e.g., parents stopping by unscheduled to speak with teachers before or after school or parents dropping off or picking up their students from school) but did not attend formal parent meetings or conferences. During the classroom observations, I jotted notes in a notebook which I then translated into typed field notes. These jottings yielded 10 to 18 pages of single-spaced typed field notes per observation for a total of 295 pages of field notes from City Charter and 249 pages of field notes from Oak Grove Elementary.

My role in the classroom was primarily one of observer. I did not discipline students or help them with their academic work. Occasionally, I took on the role of "responsible adult," staying in the classroom with a student who was missing recess while a teacher took the rest of the class to the playground. I also helped teachers occasionally with the preparation of materials for a lesson. At City Charter, my role as a "research observer" seemed to be a familiar one to students and teachers. City Charter is well regarded for its academic record as well as its approach to social and emotional learning, and I learned from a lead teacher and an administrator that the school frequently receives requests to observe its classrooms. During the time I spent at City Charter school, I was joined several times by other observers, most of whom were student teachers or teachers from other schools. One day as I prepared to enter a first grade class-room where I had observed several times before, a student in the classroom stopped me to inform me that "there are two today." Sure enough, as we walked into the classroom, I observed a middle-aged woman sitting in a chair where I usually sit writing in a small notebook.

During my process of entering the field at City Charter, I encountered the challenge of learning and adapting to the school's culture, which heavily empha-sized autonomy and self-regulation among its students. After several observa-tions in different classrooms, I began to pick up on a common language and common approach for fostering students' abilities to solve problems indepen-dently. When students occasionally asked me for assistance, I found myself trying to suppress my initial urge to directly meet their need and to imagine what a teacher at City Charter might say. I describe one of these instances in my field notes during my fifth observation in a first grade classroom:

"Excuse me, my computer isn't working," a girl says, standing in front of me. I bite back what my natural response would be [to help her] and it takes most of my willpower to stay in my seat and think about what the appropriate response is. "What do you usually do?" I ask her. "Ask Ms. Kelly but she's busy," the girl says gesturing to where her teacher is sitting at a table with Bryan and Tanya. "What other choices do you have?" I ask her. "Well, sometimes we read," she says. "That sounds like a good choice to me," I say.

In using the language of choice, I was attempting to emulate what I had heard teachers at City Charter say when encouraging students to make "smart choices" or to find "smart spots" in which to work. While the interactions between teachers and students at City Charter seemed easy and effortless, these interactional moments when I attempted to integrate myself into the culture of City Charter reminded me that this work was not effortless and instead could be characterized as a form of caring labor.

At Oak Grove Elementary, in contrast, my role as a "research observer" appeared to be an unfamiliar one. Teachers at Oak Grove Elementary were more likely to ask me if I wanted copies of their lesson plans or had questions about students' academic work as if they assumed I was there to assess their pedagogical skills or content knowledge. Across different classrooms at Oak Grove Elementary, students also expressed amazement that I was "still there" when they saw me still present in their classroom after lunch. These interactions led me to believe that most observations at this school were conducted in a context of evaluation and tended to be brief in nature. This belief was further confirmed in conversations with teachers about the school's new evaluation system which required frequent evaluations from the school's administrators. Due to the large number of teachers relative to administrators, these evaluations were usually conducted for a brief period of time.

My presence as an observer at Oak Grove Elementary also appeared to cause some discomfort for some teachers and students. Three of the teachers whom I observed expressed worry to me, in different ways, about my presence as an observer in their classroom. During my initial observation in her classroom, a first-year teacher apologized to me several times for not being as prepared as she would have liked to be for the observation. A veteran teacher, also during my initial observation, asked me several times what I would be observing in her classroom and then joked that she would "try to keep it clean." Several students also expressed curiosity or fear about what I was jotting in my notebook. One afternoon in a third grade classroom, when a teacher had stepped out of the classroom for a moment, a student asked me why I was observing in their classroom. After I explained that I was learning what it was like to be a teacher, another student seemed to be relieved as she told me that she thought I was writing down the names of students who were misbehaving.

Not all of my interactions with students at Oak Grove Elementary were characterized by feelings of discomfort or wariness, however. In one first grade classroom, I regularly received hugs from several girls in the classroom, and I came home after a February observation with several handmade Valentines from these students. On several occasions, students from the different classrooms I observed greeted me after school, asking me when I would be back to visit their classrooms. One strategy that seemed to make a difference at Oak Grove Elementary was the ability to introduce myself to students at the beginning of the observation period and to describe my project in kid-friendly terms. All teachers offered this option, but in some instances both the teachers and I forgot that we had agreed to do this, which may have contributed to some students' confusion and/or mistrust.

As a school that had continually fallen short of meeting school reform targets, the teachers at Oak Grove Elementary were under surveillance from their school district and subject to unannounced observations from members of the school district's regional office. In this context, I came to understand the tension between teachers' desire to be helpful to me and my research project and their discomfort with outside observers. As I entered and adjusted to the field at Oak Grove Elementary, I made extra efforts to establish rapport with the teachers whose classrooms I observed, spending time talking with teachers during their lunch breaks or styling myself as a sympathetic adult ear when teachers needed a moment to vent about a school practice or school reform policy. I also attempted to sit in a location in teachers' classrooms where they would be less likely to see me jotting notes and would take a break from my jottings in moments when it felt important to communicate my role as an empathetic rather than evaluative observer.

Interviews

Toward the end of the observation period, I also asked teachers for permission to interview them about their work. Several interview questions were adapted from Cohn and Kottkamp's and Lortie's studies of teachers' work.[2] The semistructured interviews were designed to collect information about what motivates teachers to teach, the work they perform inside and outside the school day, and their perceptions of this work. During the interviews, I also asked teachers to reflect on particular instances of student challenges or care work that I observed in the classroom. I supplemented these interviews with conversations with administrators and school support staff. After each interview, the participants completed a brief demographic questionnaire, which is based on the National Schools and Staffing Survey.[3] Once the interviews for a single school had been completed, I transcribed the interviews with the aid of Express Scribe transcription software and transferred the information from the demographic questionnaires to an Excel document for analysis.

Public elementary school teachers across the nation predominantly identify as White and female, and my sample of teachers reflected this trend.[4] All but one of my nineteen interview participants were female, and the male participant was an administrator. Four participants identified as Black/African American, one identified as Latino/Hispanic, one identified as Asian, and the remainder identified as White. My sample was relatively young, with most participants under the age of thirty-five, three between the ages of thirty-five and forty-nine, and two aged fifty or older. One of my interview participants worked in a kindergarten classroom, five worked in first grade classrooms, five worked in second grade classrooms, four worked in third grade classrooms, and four worked in administration or support positions. The demographic characteristics at the two schools were very similar in terms of teachers' race and ethnicity and the grade levels that I observed. Teachers who I observed at City Charter were, on average, younger than the teachers I observed at Oak Grove Elementary.

Another difference between the teachers I interviewed at Oak Grove Elementary and City Charter was their pathway to becoming teachers. All but one of the teachers whom I interviewed at City Charter had come to teaching through an alternative certification program, such as Teach For America. Most teachers had studied a subject other than education in college, usually public policy, and were motivated to teach by an interest in "making a difference" or addressing particular forms of educational inequality. Most teachers at City Charter also were not planning to remain working as a classroom teacher for their entire career. In contrast, all but one of the teachers at Oak Grove Elementary had studied education in college and had become certified to teach through a traditional route. Teachers at Oak Grove Elementary were more likely to talk about teaching as a career to which they were committed and, in some cases, had been committed to since an early age. This difference may also have played a role in teachers' comfort level with outside observers.

Informed Consent and Confidentiality

Prior to each interview, I obtained written consent from participants to conduct the interview and to audio record it. When scheduling and confirming interviews with teachers, I typically sent them an electronic copy of the consent form to review and then brought hard copies of the written consent form to the interview so that teachers would also have the option of keeping a hard copy of the consent form for their files. I responded to any questions that teachers had about the consent form and secured their signature before beginning the interview. All but two participants (a lead teacher and an administrator, both at Oak Grove Elementary) agreed to have their interviews audio-recorded. I maintained participants' confidentiality through the use of codes as identifiers on all audio files, interview transcripts, and classroom observation notes. When sharing direct quotations, I have used pseudonyms to protect the confidentiality of research participants and to maintain the anonymity of the schools where I conducted my research.

I initially planned to disclose the specific city and suburb in which I conducted my research, and I received permission from the traditional public school's IRB office to do so. However, after I completed an initial analysis of the data, I realized that the level of detail I provided in describing the social organization of City Charter School could compromise the anonymity of the school, as it is well known in its district for several of these characteristics, including its approach to social and emotional learning. Since this aspect of City Charter was so relevant to my study, I decided to err on the side of greater anonymity in describing the geographic context so that I could provide a more detailed analysis of the school's social organization.

Data Analysis

The data analysis procedures for this study employed techniques associated with modified analytic induction[5] and closely followed Esterberg's guide for qualitative data analysis.[6] The data analysis methods for this study also drew on the practices of institutional ethnography, moving from the local (i.e., specific instances of teachers' care work) to the extra-local (i.e., how school organization and school reform policies constrain and enable teachers' care work).

In the first phase of data analysis, I sought to identify aspects of teachers' noninstructional work that were oriented to meeting students' social, emotional, and material needs. To do this, I first engaged in a process of open coding, reading through hard copies of field notes and interview transcripts and jotting notes in the margins about themes that were emerging that could be used as potential codes. These codes included examples of care work that have already been identified in the literature (e.g., building rapport with students), examples that did not fit within existing conceptual categories (e.g., restorative justice approaches), and the absence of particular types of care work in a given setting.

Once I had a list of potential codes, I narrowed down this list, removing or revising codes that were duplicative or overlapped conceptually. I used this narrower list of codes to engage in a process of focused coding, reading through field notes and interview transcripts again, this time with a set of highlighters, highlighting sections of text that corresponded to the codes I had identified. After several rounds of focused coding, I organized my data electronically, using a Word document. Here, I cut and pasted the text I had highlighted and organized it into major coding themes and subthemes. For example, one of my major coding themes was "relational care" and subcodes for this theme included "developing rapport" and "recognition and acknowledgement." I further refined some of these subcodes to focus on the specific ways that teachers sought to develop rapport or recognize students, such as joking with students, asking students about their lives outside school, and providing formal incentives to reward students for good behavior. I completed this initial data analysis sepa-rately for each school following the completion of data collection at each school.

When I compared the noninstructional work that teachers performed at the two school sites, it became clear that the types of care work that teachers engaged in differed significantly between the two schools. The second step of my data analysis sought to account for these differences and examine their implications. This time, I decided not to reprint over 500 pages of field notes and interview transcripts and instead completed the same open and focused coding process electronically. I identified themes related to the noncognitive skills that were being transmitted to students and aspects of the social organization of the schools that contributed to the transmission of particular noncognitive skills. For example, when identifying the noncognitive skills that were transmitted at City Charter School, I developed general codes such as "negotiation and problem-solving," "logical consequences," and "self-regulation." After the cod-ing categories had been refined and applied to the data, I coded within these categories to identify the specific practices that were associated with the trans-mission of these noncognitive skills. These coding categories included specific classroom practices such as "morning meetings," "smart spots," and "must do's." When I completed the open and focused coding for both schools, I then organized the data similarly to the first phase of my data analysis, cut-ting and pasting coded data into a Word document that was organized based on major coding themes and subthemes.

Strengths and Limitations of the Study Design

The multisite nature of this study allowed me to examine the relationship between school reform policies, care work, and the transmission of noncogni-tive skills within two very different school contexts. Multisite studies are appro-priate for research designs that seek to demonstrate generalizability or diversity.[7] In this study, the purpose of conducting research at more than one site was to maximize diversity—to compare and contrast the noninstructional work that teachers perform within different school contexts. "The more cases included in a study, and the greater variation across the cases, the more com-pelling an interpretation is likely to be."[8] In the case of this study, there were several important differences between Oak Grove Elementary and City Char-ter: the degree to which they met their school district's school reform mandates; the structure of the school (public vs. charter) and the degree of autonomy that structure afforded; and the culture and social organization of the schools. In the book's chapters, I describe how these contrasting factors are related and how they influence the noncognitive skills that are transmitted to students.

Examining two schools that are, in some respects, very different than each other also provides an opportunity for a more nuanced examination of the influence of school reform policies in what has become a very polarized school reform context. As this study demonstrates, Oak Grove Elementary and City Charter have much to teach us about the perils and possibilities of school reform policies. At the same time, I would caution readers from generalizing from the examples of these two schools to all public charter schools or all traditional public schools. Not all public charter schools are academically successful, as the research cited in the introduction demonstrates. Traditional public schools have also experimented with the types of social and emotional learning programs espoused by City Charter. Where there may be opportunities to generalize (and, in order to do so, further research should be conducted), this would be regarding the existence of an interconnected set of conditions. For example, based on the experiences of teachers at Oak Grove Elementary, could we expect other traditional public schools, who have repeatedly been informed they have failed to meet school reform mandates and who are under frequent surveillance from their school district, to focus intently on protecting the boundaries of the "learning day" and to transmit noncognitive skills focused on compliance and deference? If so, what might this tell us about the potential unintended consequences of school reform policies in these contexts?

In addition to including more than one site of analysis in my study, I also sought to strengthen my research design by including more than one data source. I included classroom observations, teacher interviews, and a demographic survey in an effort to create a richer and more comprehensive account of the relationship between school reform policies, care work, and the transmission of noncognitive skills. Having access to multiple data sources provided me with the opportunity to engage in the process of triangulation, the practice of combining multiple methods to study the same phenomenon, a key practice in enhancing the credibility of qualitative studies.[9] Combining classroom observations and interviews also aided my data collection process by allowing me to develop a measure of rapport with teachers during observations that I was able to draw on in the interviews. A recent study of teacher development and retention found that "[f]rom a methodological standpoint, classroom observations also enabled deeper and more robust interviewing: The observation experience built additional trust between interviewer and interviewee and offered concrete material for the subsequent (and directly following) interviews."[10]

The cross-sectional nature of my design proved limiting in assessing the long-term effects of the transmission of noncognitive skills to students. While I can raise questions and discuss potential implications about the likely effects of the transmission of different sets of noncognitive skills to students at Oak Grove Elementary and City Charter, future research is needed to examine the extent to which noncognitive skills taught to students in elementary school persist beyond the elementary school years.

Acknowledgments

The seeds for this book were planted when I was a child listening to my mother and aunt talk about their work in public schools during family dinners, where autonomy and constraints on autonomy were a common theme, and during the year I taught third grade in a public elementary school as part of the Teach for America program. The research for this book was supported by my dissertation advisor, Amy Best, and dissertation committee members Karen Rosenblum, Diana D'Amico, and Hava Gordon, who provided encouragement and feedback throughout the research process; by the many people who helped connect me with teachers and administrators during the recruitment phase of this project, including Sarah Leonard, Lauren McAlee, Susan McKinley, Jane Woodburn, and teachers at City Charter and Oak Grove Elementary; by the members of the institutional review board in Oak Grove Elementary's school district and school administrators at both schools who allowed me to conduct research in their schools; and by George Mason University's Office of the Provost, which provided several fellowships that helped to fund this project. This research became a book with the support of Executive Editor Peter Mickulas and Series Editor Lisa Nunn and with helpful and insightful feedback from anonymous reviewers and from colleagues, including Drew Bonner, Carlos Coleman, Randy Lynn, and Sara Moore. This book would not exist without the generosity, energy, and heart of the teachers and students at Oak Grove Elementary and City Charter, who welcomed me into their classrooms and demonstrated what care looked like on a daily basis.

Notes

Introduction

1   As is discussed in more detail in this introduction and the appendix, I have chosen to describe teachers and students as I perceived them in the field and, in the case of teachers, how they described their gender, racial, and ethnic identities in a demographic survey. I did not distribute a demographic survey to students, so I have relied on my own observations and the pronouns used by teachers and students to characterize students' racial, ethnic, and gender identities. This strategy has its limitations—given the choice, students may have emphasized aspects of their identity that I did not, corrected pronouns used by others, or de-emphasized aspects of their identity that I highlighted. In describing students' racial identities I have used the term Black to encompass students who may have identified as African American, Caribbean American, or African.

2   Southern Education Foundation, "A New Majority: Low Income Students Now a Majority in the Nation's Public Schools. Research Bulletin," 2015, https:// https:// files.eric.ed.gov/fulltext/ED555829.pdf.

3   No Kid Hungry, "Hunger in Our Schools," 2015, https://www.hungerinour schools.org.

4   Elizabeth McNichol et al., *Pulling Apart: A State-by-State Analysis of Income Trends* (Washington, DC: Economic Policy Institute, 2012), https://www.epi.org /publication/studies_pullingapart/; Carmen Denavas-Walt, Bernadette D. Proctor, and Jessica C. Smith, "Income, Poverty, and Health Insurance Coverage in the United States: 2009," *United States Census Bureau*, Report P60-238, September 1, 2010, https://www.census.gov/library/publications/2010/demo/p60-238.html; Douglas S. Massey, *Categorically Unequal: The American Stratification System* (New York: Russell Sage Foundation, 2007).

5   See Katharine Alaimo, Christine M. Olsen, and Edward A. Frongillo, "Food Insufficiency and American School-Aged Children's Cognitive, Academic, and Psychosocial Development," *Pediatrics* 108, no.1 (2001): 44–53; Linda Weinreb et al., "Hunger: Its Impact on Children's Health and Mental Health," *Pediatrics* 110, no. 4 (2002): 1–9; Joshua Winicki and Kyle Jemison, "Food Insecurity and Hunger in the Kindergarten Classroom: Its Effect on Learning and Growth,"

Contemporary Economic Policy 21, no. 2 (2003): 145–157; Karen F. Osterman, "Students' Need for Belonging in the School Community," *Review of Educational Research* 70, no. 3 (September 1, 2000): 323–367, https://doi.org/10.3102/00346543 070003323.

6 U.S. Department of Education, "Executive Summary of the No Child Left Behind Act of 2001," Legislative Materials, Abstracts, November 20, 2007, http://www2 .ed.gov/nclb/overview/intro/execsumm.html.

7 U.S. Department of Education, "Executive Summary."

8 U.S. Department of Education, "Executive Summary."

9 U.S. Department of Education, "Executive Summary."

10 U.S. Department of Education, "Race to the Top Program: Executive Summary," Washington, DC, November 2009, http://www2.ed.gov/programs/racetothetop /executive-summary.pdf.

11 "Race to the Top," U.S. Department of Education, 12.

12 Deborah Greenblatt, "The Consequences of edTPA," *Educational Leadership* 73, no. 8 (May 2016): 51–54.

13 Claudio Sanchez, "Obama's Impact on America's Schools," NPR, 2017, https://www .npr.org/sections/ed/2017/01/13/500421608/obamas-impact-on-americas-schools.

14 National Center for Education Statistics, "Public Charter School Enrollment," 2020, https://nces.ed.gov/programs/coe/indicator_cgb.asp.

15 Dennis Epple, Richard Romano, and Ron Zimmer, "Charter Schools: Research on Their Characteristics and Effectiveness," 2015, National Bureau of Economic Research Working Paper 21256, https://www.nber.org/system/files/working _papers/w21256/w21256.pdf.

16 Epple et al., "Charter Schools," p. 29.

17 Epple et al., "Charter Schools." For additional perspectives on charter schools and school segregation, see Iris C. Rothberg and Joshua L. Glazer, eds., *Choosing Charters: Better Schools or More Segregation* (New York: Teachers College Press, 2018).

18 Edward Cremata et al., "National Charter School Study," CREDO, 2013, https:// credo.stanford.edu/sites/g/files/sbiybj6481/f/ncss_2013_final_draft.pdf.

19 Amy Stuart Wells et al., "Charter Schools as Postmodern Paradox: Rethinking Social Stratification in an Age of Deregulated School Choice," *Harvard Educational Review* 69, no. 2 (December 31, 2009): 175, https://doi.org/10.17763/haer.69.2.k34 475n478v43022.

20 Jason Richardson, Bruce Mitchell, and Juan Franco, National Community Reinvestment Coalition, "Shifting Neighborhoods: Gentrification and Cultural Displacement in American Cities," 2019, https://ncrc.org/gentrification/.

21 Center for Responsive Schools, "About Responsive Classroom: The Four Key Domains of Responsive Classroom," 2021, https://www.responsiveclassroom.org /about/.

22 Elizabeth McNichol et al., *Pulling Apart*; U.S. Census Bureau, *Income, Poverty, and Health Insurance*.

23 Department of Agriculture Food and Nutrition Service, "Child Nutrition Programs: Income Eligibility Guidelines," *Federal Register* 77, no. 5 (March 23, 2012), https://www.govinfo.gov/app/details/FR-2012-03-23/2012-7036.

24 U.S. Census Bureau, *Income, Poverty, and Health Insurance*.

25 McNichol et al., *Pulling Apart*.

26 Winicki and Jemison, "Food Insecurity and Hunger."

27 Alaimo et al., "Food Insufficiency."

28 Alaimo et al., "Food Insufficiency."

29   Charles E. Basch, "Vision and the Achievement Gap Among Urban Minority Youth," *School Health* 81, no. 10 (2011): 599–605; Stephanie L. Jackson et al., "Impact of Poor Oral Health on Children's School Attendance and Performance," *American Journal of Public Health* 101, no. 10 (October 1, 2011): 1900–1906, doi:10.2105/AJPH.2010.200915.

30   Donna R. Sanderson, "Transiency, Test Scores, and the Public: One School District's Story," *Studies in Educational Evaluation* 30, no. 3 (2004): 225–236.

31   Charles E. Basch, "Breakfast and the Achievement Gap Among Urban Minority Youth," *School Health* 81, no. 10 (2011): 635–640.

32   Food Research and Action Center, "Community Eligibility," 2021, https://frac .org/community-eligibility.

33   Amelie A. Hecht, Keshia M. Pollack Porter, and Lindsay Turner, "Impact of The Community Eligibility Provision of the Healthy, Hunger-Free Kids Act on Student Nutrition, Behavior, and Academic Outcomes: 2011–2019," *AJPH* (August 12, 2020): https://ajph.aphapublications.org/doi/10.2105/AJPH.2020.305743.

34   While Oak Grove Elementary and City Charter did not identify as Community Schools, their attention to meeting students' material needs is characteristic of the Community Schools approach, which promotes parent engagement, shared leadership, and coordination with community healthcare, social service, and recreational resources to support a more holistic approach to education. For more information about Community Schools, see Marieke Heers et al., "Community Schools: What We Know and What We Need to Know," *Review of Educational Research* (December 1, 2016), doi: 10.3102/0034654315627365; Anna Maier et al., "Community Schools as an Effective School Improvement Strategy: A Review of the Evidence," Learning Policy Institute, Palo Alto, CA, 2017, https://files.eric .ed.gov/fulltext/ED606765.pdf.

35   American School Counselor Association, "State School Counseling Mandates and Legislation," 2017, https://www.schoolcounselor.org/About-School-Counseling/ State-Requirements-Programs/State-School-Counseling-Mandates-Legislation.

36   National Center for Education Statistics, "School Nurses in U.S. Public Schools," U.S. Department of Education, Washington, DC, April 30, 2020, https://nces .ed.gov/pubsearch/pubsinfo.asp?pubid=2020086.

37   Susan Levine, *School Lunch Politics: The Surprising History of America's Favorite Welfare Program* (Princeton, NJ: Princeton University Press, 2010), https://press .princeton.edu/books/paperback/9780691146195/school-lunch-politics.

38   Levine, *School Lunch Politics*.

39   Joshua Bloom and Waldo E. Martin, *Black Against Empire: The History and Politics of the Black Panther Party* (Oakland: University of California Press, 2016); Levine, *School Lunch Politics*.

40   Dorothy E. Smith, *Institutional Ethnography: A Sociology for People*, The Gender Lens Series (Walnut Creek, CA: AltaMira, 2005).

41   Hava Rachel Gordon, "'We Can't Let Them Fail for One More Day': School Reform Urgency and the Politics of Reformer-Community Alliances," *Race Ethnicity and Education* 19, no. 1 (January 2, 2016): 1–22, https://doi.org/10.1080 /13613324.2014.885430.

42   Jean Anyon, "Social Class and the Hidden Curriculum of Work," *Journal of Education* 162, no. 1 (1980): 67–92.

43   Gordon, "We Can't Let Them Fail for One More Day"; Kenneth J. Saltman, *Capitalizing on Disaster: Taking and Breaking Public Schools*, Cultural Politics & the Promise of Democracy (Boulder, CO: Paradigm, 2007).

Chapter 1   Beyond Standardized Testing

1 Joan C. Tronto, *Caring Democracy: Markets, Equality, and Justice* (New York: New York University Press, 2013).
2 David E. Frisvold, "Nutrition and Cognitive Achievement: An Evaluation of the School Breakfast Program," *Journal of Public Economics* 124 (2015): 91–104; R. E. Kleinman et al., "Diet, Breakfast, and Academic Performance in Children," *Annals of Nutrition & Metabolism* 46, no. 1 (2002): 24–30; Alan F. Meyers et al., "School Breakfast Program and School Performance," *American Journal of Diseases of Children* 143, no. 10 (1989): 1234–1239.
3 Charles E. Basch, "Breakfast and the Achievement Gap Among Urban Minority Youth," *Journal of School Health* 81, no. 10 (2011): 635–640.
4 Basch, "Breakfast and the Achievement Gap."
5 Basch, "Breakfast and the Achievement Gap."
6 Lorraine M. Gutiérrez and Edith A. Lewis, *Empowering Women of Color* (New York: Columbia University Press, 1999).
7 Gutiérrez and Lewis, *Empowering Women of Color*; Jerome H. Schiele, M. Sebrena Jackson, and Colita Nichols Fairfax, "Maggie Lena Walker and African American Community Development," *Affilia* 20, no. 1 (February 1, 2005): 21–38, https://doi.org/10.1177/0886109904272012; Caroline Shenaz Hossein, "The Politics of Resistance: Informal Banks in the Caribbean," *Review of Black Political Economy* 41, no. 1 (January 1, 2014): 85–100, https://doi.org/10.1007/s12114-013-9171-9.
8 While City Charter did not identify as a Community School, there were aspects of the school's organization that reflected principles of Community Schools, including the presence of a full-time school nurse and a full-time social worker. For more information about Community Schools, see: Marieke Heers et al., "Community Schools: What We Know and What We Need to Know," *Review of Educational Research* (December 1, 2016), doi: 10.3102/0034654315627365; and Anna Maier et al., "Community Schools as an Effective School Improvement Strategy: A Review of the Evidence," Learning Policy Institute, Palo Alto, CA, 2017, https://files.eric.ed.gov/fulltext/ED606765.pdf.
9 Geneva Gay, *Culturally Responsive Teaching: Theory, Research, and Practice*, 2nd ed. (New York: Teachers College Press, 2010); Gloria Ladson-Billings, "Toward a Theory of Culturally Relevant Pedagogy," *American Educational Research Journal* 32, no. 3 (September 1, 1995): 465–491, https://doi.org/10.3102/00028312032003465.

Chapter 2   Working in an Audit Culture

1 U.S. Department of Education, "Race to the Top Program: Executive Summary," Washington, DC, November 2009, http://www2.ed.gov/programs/racetothetop/executive-summary.pdf.
2 U.S. Department of Education, "Race to the Top," 12.
3 Cris Shore, "Audit Culture and Illiberal Governance: Universities and the Politics of Accountability," *Anthropological Theory* 8, no. 3 (September 1, 2008): 279, https://doi.org/10.1177/1463499608093815.
4 Shore, "Audit Culture and Illiberal Governance."
5 Michael Power, "Making Things Auditable," *Accounting, Organizations and Society* 21, no. 2–3 (February 1, 1996): 289–315, https://doi.org/10.1016/0361-3682(95)00004-6.
6 Shore, "Audit Culture and Illiberal Governance," 281.

7   Michael W. Apple, "Education, Markets, and an Audit Culture," *Critical Quarterly* 47, no. 1–2 (July 2005): 11–29, https://doi.org/10.1111/j.0011-1562.2005 .00611.x.

8   S. K. Biklen, *School Work: Gender and the Cultural Construction of Teaching* (New York: Teachers College Press, 1995). The association of teaching with "women's work" was also a racialized process as the "cult of true womanhood" (Collins 2000) moved into the public sphere, positioning White middle-class women as ideal mothers and teachers.

9   Russell J. Skiba, Mariella I. Arredondo, and Natasha T. Williams, "More Than a Metaphor: The Contribution of Exclusionary Discipline to a School-to-Prison Pipeline," *Equity & Excellence in Education* 47, no. 4 (2014): 546–564, https://doi .org/10.1080/10665684.2014.958965. Race and gender intersect here as well. Black girls experience racialized forms of surveillance that are different than those experienced by young Black men, just as Latina youth experience different forms of oppression than do Latino youth. See Dorinda J. Carter Andrews et al., "The Impossibility of Being 'Perfect and White': Black Girls' Racialized and Gendered Schooling Experiences," *American Educational Research Journal* 56, no. 6 (December 2019): 2531–2572; Julio Cammarota, "The Gendered and Racialized Pathways of Latina and Latino Youth: Different Struggles, Different Resistances in the Urban Context" *Anthropology and Education Quarterly* 35, no. 1 (2004): 53–74.

10 U.S. Department of Education, "Title I, Part A Fact Sheet," Pamphlets, March 9, 2006, https://www2.ed.gov/rschstat/eval/disadv/title1-factsheet.html?exp=0.

11 U. S. Government Accountability Office, "No Child Left Behind Act: Education Should Clarify Guidance and Address Potential Compliance Issues for Schools in Corrective Action and Restructuring Status," no. GAO-07-1035, September 5, 2007), https://www.gao.gov/products/GAO-07-1035.

12 Scholastic and Bill and Melinda Gates Foundation, "Primary Sources: America's Teachers on Teaching in an Era of Change," 3rd ed., Scholastic Inc. and the Bill & Melinda Gates Foundation, 2013, https://eric.ed.gov/?id=ED562664.

13 Cassandra M. Guarino, Lucrecia Santibañez, and Glenn A. Daley, "Teacher Recruitment and Retention: A Review of the Recent Empirical Literature," *Review of Educational Research* 76, no. 2 (June 1, 2006): 173–208, https://doi.org/10.3102 /00346543076002173.

14 Guarino et al., "Teacher Recruitment and Retention."

15 Dorothea Anagnostopoulos, "The New Accountability, Student Failure, and Teachers' Work in Urban High Schools," *Educational Policy* 17, no. 3 (July 2003): 291–316.

16 Scholastic and Bill and Melinda Gates Foundation, "Primary Sources."

17 Lora Bartlett, "Expanding Teacher Work Roles: A Resource for Retention or a Recipe for Overwork?" *Journal of Education Policy* 19, no. 5 (September 2004), 567.

18 Bartlett, "Expanding Teacher Work Roles," 568.

Chapter 3   "This is the Most Dreadful Test"

1   Jean Anyon, "Social Class and the Hidden Curriculum of Work," *Journal of Education* 162, no. 1 (1980): 67–92.

2   Anyon, "Social Class," 89–90.

3 Brittany Aronson and Judson Laughter, "The Theory and Practice of Culturally Relevant Education: A Synthesis of Research Across Content Areas," *Review of Educational Research* 86, no. 1 (March 1, 2016): 163–206, https://doi.org/10.3102 /0034654315582066.

4 Geneva Gay, *Culturally Responsive Teaching: Theory, Research, and Practice,* 2nd ed. (New York: Teachers College Press, 2010).

5 Geneva Gay, "Preparing for Culturally Responsive Teaching," *Journal of Teacher Education* 53, no. 2 (March 1, 2002), 110, https://doi.org/10.1177/00224871020530 02003.

6 Gloria Ladson-Billings, "Toward a Theory of Culturally Relevant Pedagogy," *American Education Research Journal* 32, no. 3 (1995): 465–491.

7 Ladson-Billings, "Toward a Theory of Culturally Relevant Pedagogy."

8 Ladson-Billings, "Toward a Theory of Culturally Relevant Pedagogy," 481.

9 As Michelle Hughes and Whitney Tucker note, "A variety of childhood adversities have a root cause in family economic insufficiency, indicating that poverty may likely be the first adversity that many children experience. Poverty acts as a reinforcing mechanism, disproportionately burdening low-income families with stressors that give rise to adverse conditions, which then convey additional stress and cognitive dysfunction. The devastating effect of this negative feedback loop on the development of children is well documented, and childhood poverty has been strongly linked to a variety of negative outcomes across the life course, including low educational attainment, increased exposure to violence, hunger, parental incarceration, and increased likelihood of being subject to abuse and neglect." Michelle Hughes and Whitney Tucker, "Poverty as an Adverse Childhood Experience," *NCMJ* 79, no. 2 (2018), 124.

10 M. Shelley Thomas, Shantel Crosby, and Judi Vanderhaar, "Trauma-Informed Practices in Schools Across Two Decades: An Interdisciplinary Review of Research," *Review of Research in Education* 43 (March 2019): 422–452.

11 Kimberly L. Oliver and Rosary Lalik, "The Body as Curriculum: Learning with Adolescent Girls," *Journal of Curriculum Studies* 33, no. 3 (May 1, 2001): 303–333, https://doi.org/10.1080/00220270010006046.

Chapter 4   Working as Part of a School Reform Movement

1 U.S. Department of Education, "No Child Left Behind: A Toolkit for Teachers," Pamphlets, U.S. Department of Education, August 13, 2009, https://files.eric .ed.gov/fulltext/ED483139.pdf.

2 U.S. Department of Education, "No Child Left Behind."

3 Teach For America, "Internships and College Programs," 2021, https://www .teachforamerica.org/how-to-join/internships-and-college-programs.

4 National Center for Education Statistics, "Schools and Staffing Survey (SASS)," 2013, http://nces.ed.gov/surveys/sass/index.asp.

5 Daniel C. Humphrey and Marjorie E. Wechsler, "Insights into Alternative Certification: Initial Findings from a National Study," *Teachers College Record* 109, no. 3 (2007): 483–530.

6 National Center for Education Statistics, "Characteristics of Public School Teachers Who Completed Alternative Route to Certification Programs," *Condition of Education,* U.S. Department of Education, Institute of Education Sciences, Washington, DC, 2018, https://nces.ed.gov/programs/coe/indicator_tlc.asp.

7 National Center for Education Statistics, "Racial/Ethnic Enrollment in Public Schools," *Condition of Education*, U.S. Department of Education, Institute of Education Sciences, Washington, DC, 2020, https://nces.ed.gov/programs/coe/indicator_cge.asp.

8 National Center for Education Statistics, "Characteristics of Public School Teachers," *Condition of Education*, U.S. Department of Education, Institute of Education Sciences, Washington, DC, 2020, https://nces.ed.gov/programs/coe/indicator_clr.asp.

9 National Center for Education Statistics, "Characteristics of Public School Teachers Who Completed Alternative Route to Certification Programs."

10 Julian Vasquez Heilig and Su Jin Jez, "Teach For America: A Return to the Evidence," National Education Policy Center, University of Colorado Boulder, January 2014, https://nepc.colorado.edu/sites/default/files/tfa-return_0.pdf.

11 Ashlee Anderson, "Teach for America and the Dangers of Deficit Thinking," *Critical Education* 4, no. 11 (October 15, 2013), https://doi.org/10.14288/ce.v4i11.183936; Ashlee Anderson, "Teach for America and Symbolic Violence: A Bourdieuian Analysis of Education's Next Quick-Fix," *Urban Review* 45, no. 5 (December 1, 2013): 684–700, https://doi.org/10.1007/s11256-013-0241-x.

12 Colette N. Cann, "What School Movies and TFA Teach Us About Who Should Teach Urban Youth: Dominant Narratives as Public Pedagogy," *Urban Education* 50, no. 3 (April 1, 2015): 288–315, https://doi.org/10.1177/0042085913507458.

13 Teach For America, "What We Do," 2021, https://www.teachforamerica.org/what-we-do.

14 Julian Vasquez Heilig and Su Jin Jez, "Teach For America: A Review of the Evidence," National Education Policy Center, Boulder, CO, 2010, http://nepc.colorado.edu/publication/teach-for-america.

15 Heilig and Jez, "A Review of the Evidence."

16 Heilig and Jez, "A Return to the Evidence," i.

17 Hava Rachel Gordon, "'We Can't Let Them Fail for One More Day': School Reform Urgency and the Politics of Reformer-Community Alliances," *Race Ethnicity and Education* 19, no. 1 (January 2, 2016): 1–22, https://doi.org/10.1080/13613324.2014.885430; Kenneth J. Saltman, *Capitalizing on Disaster: Taking and Breaking Public Schools.* Cultural Politics & the Promise of Democracy (Boulder, CO: Paradigm, 2007).

18 Gordon, "We Can't Let Them Fail for One More Day."

19 Prudence L. Carter and Kevin G. Welner, eds., *Closing the Opportunity Gap: What America Must Do to Give Every Child an Even Chance* (Oxford: Oxford University Press, 2013).

20 Kevin G. Welner and Prudence L. Carter, "Achievement Gaps Arise from Opportunity Gaps," in *Closing the Opportunity Gap: What America Must Do to Give Every Child an Even Chance*, eds. Prudence L. Carter and Kevin G. Welner (Oxford: Oxford University Press, 2013), 3.

21 By gendered labor, I am referring to the cultural construction of teaching as "women's work," specifically White middle-class women's work, that began in the nineteenth century in the United States. Men were more likely to hold teaching positions until the mid-nineteenth century, when women assumed primary responsibility for educating students in primary and secondary schools in the United States. Scholars have attributed the feminization of teaching to social and economic transformations related to industrialization, including a new household

division of labor in white middle-class households that changed the types of work women were expected to pursue and the cultural meanings associated with this work. See M. Carnoy and H. M. Levin, *Schooling and Work in the Democratic State* (Stanford, CA: Stanford University Press, 1985); J. A. Preston, "Domestic Ideology, School Reformers, and Female Teachers: Schoolteaching Becomes Women's Work in Nineteenth-Century New England," *New England Quarterly* 66, no. 4 (1993): 531–551; and J. L. Rury, "Who Became Teachers? The Social Characteristics of Teachers in American History," in *American Teachers: Histories of a Profession at Work*, ed. D. R. Warren (New York: Macmillan, 1989): 9–48.

22   Timothy Diamond, *Making Gray Gold: Narratives of Nursing Home Care* (Chicago: University of Chicago Press, 1995).

23   Mignon Duffy, *Making Care Count: A Century of Gender, Race, and Paid Care Work* (New Brunswick, NJ: Rutgers University Press, 2011), 61.

24   National Alliance for Public Charter Schools, "Unionized Charter Schools: Data from 2018–2019," Washington, DC, December 18, 2020, https://www.publicchar ters.org/our-work/publications/unionized-charter-schools-data-2018-2019.

Chapter 5   "I Would Love to Hear What You Have to Say"

1   Center for Responsive Schools, "About Responsive Classroom: The Four Key Domains of Responsive Classroom," 2021, https://www.responsiveclassroom.org/about/.

2   Center for Responsive Schools, "About Responsive Classroom."

3   Jean Anyon, "Social Class and the Hidden Curriculum of Work," *Journal of Education* 162, no. 1 (1980): 67–92.

4   Pierre Bourdieu and Jean-Claude Passeron, *Reproduction in Education, Society, and Culture* (Beverly Hills, CA: SAGE, 1977); Tara J. Yosso, "Whose Culture has Capital? A Critical Race Theory Discussion of Community Cultural Wealth," *Race, Ethnicity, and Education* 8, no. 1 (2005): 69–91.

5   Howard Gardner, *Frames of Mind: The Theory of Multiple Intelligences* (New York: Basic Books, 2011).

6   John D. Mayer, Richard D. Roberts, and Sigal G. Barsade, "Human Abilities: Emotional Intelligence," *Annual Review of Psychology* 59, no. 1 (2008): 511, https://doi.org/10.1146/annurev.psych.59.103006.093646.

7   Peter Salovey and Daisy Grewal, "The Science of Emotional Intelligence," *Current Directions in Psychological Science* 14, no. 6 (December 1, 2005): 281–285.

8   Peter Salovey and John D. Mayer, "Emotional Intelligence," *Imagination, Cognition and Personality* 9, no. 3 (March 1, 1990): 185–211, https://doi.org/10.2190/DUGG-P24E-52WK-6CDG.

9   Daniel Goleman, *Emotional Intelligence: Why It Can Matter More Than IQ*, 10th Anniversary ed. (New York: Random House, 2012).

10   Mayer et al., "Human Abilities."

11   Susanne A. Denham et al., "Preschool Emotional Competence: Pathway to Social Competence?" *Child Development* 74, no. 1 (February 1, 2003): 238–256, https://doi.org/10.1111/1467-8624.00533; Nancy Eisenberg et al., "Dispositional Emotionality and Regulation: Their Role in Predicting Quality of Social Functioning," *Journal of Personality and Social Psychology* 78, no. 1 (2000): 136–157, https://doi.org/10.1037/0022-3514.78.1.136.

12   John D. Mayer and Casey D. Cobb, "Educational Policy on Emotional Intelligence: Does It Make Sense?" *Educational Psychology Review* 12, no. 2 (January 1, 2000): 163–183.

13 Goleman, *Emotional Intelligence*.

14 Goleman, *Emotional Intelligence*.

15 American Psychological Association Zero Tolerance Task Force, "Are Zero Tolerance Policies Effective in the Schools? An Evidentiary Review and Recommendations," *American Psychologist* 63, no. 9 (December 2008): 852–862, https://doi.org/10.1037/0003 -066X.63.9.852; Alicia Darensbourg, Erica Perez, and Jamilia J. Blake, "Overrepresentation of African American Males in Exclusionary Discipline: The Role of School-Based Mental Health Professionals in Dismantling the School to Prison Pipeline," *Journal of African American Males in Education* 1, no. 3 (2010): 196–211.

16 Belinda Hopkins, *Just Schools: A Whole School Approach to Restorative Justice* (London: Jessica Kingsley, 2003).

17 Hopkins, *Just Schools*.

18 Brenda Morrison, Peta Blood, and Margaret Thorsborne, "Practicing Restorative Justice in School Communities: Addressing the Challenge of Culture Change," *Public Organization Review* 5, no. 4 (December 14, 2005): 335–357, https://doi .org/10.1007/s11115-005-5095-6.

19 Morrison et al., "Practicing Restorative Justice in School Communities."

20 Christine A. Christie, C. Michael Nelson, and Kristine Jolivette, "School Characteristics Related to the Use of Suspension," *Education and Treatment of Children* 27, no. 4 (2004): 509–526.

21 Hilary Lustick, "'Restorative Justice' or Restoring Order? Restorative School Discipline Practices in Urban Public Schools," *Urban Education* (November 14, 2017), https://doi.org/10.1177/0042085917741725.

22 Claudia G. Vincent et al., "Discipline Referrals and Access to Secondary Level Support in Elementary and Middle Schools: Patterns Across African-American, Hispanic-American, and White Students," *Education and Treatment of Children* 35, no. 3 (2012): 431–458.

23 Annette Lareau, *Unequal Childhoods: Class, Race, and Family Life* (Berkeley: University of California Press, 2003).

24 Peter J. Collier and David L. Morgan, "'Is That Paper Really Due Today?' Differences in First-Generation and Traditional College Students' Understandings of Faculty Expectations," *Higher Education* 55, no. 4 (April 1, 2008): 425–446; Melinda Mechur Karp and Rachel Hare Bork, "'They Never Told Me What to Expect, So I Didn't Know What to Do': Defining and Clarifying the Role of a Community College Student" (CCRC Working Paper No. 47, Community College Research Center, Columbia University, New York, July 2012), http://eric.ed.gov/?id=ED535078.

25 Karp and Bork, "They Never Told Me What to Expect."

26 Collier and Morgan, "Is That Paper Really Due Today?"; Karp and Bork, "They Never Told Me What to Expect."

27 Karp and Bork, "They Never Told Me What to Expect," 13.

28 Ann Swidler, "Culture in Action: Symbols and Strategies," *American Sociological Review* 51, no. 2 (April 1, 1986): 273–286, https://doi.org/10.2307/2095521.

Appendix

1 Dorothy E. Smith, *Institutional Ethnography: A Sociology for People*, The Gender Lens Series (Walnut Creek, CA: AltaMira, 2005).

2 Marilyn M. Cohn and Robert B. Kottkamp, *Teachers: The Missing Voice in Education* (Albany: State University of New York Press, 1993); Dan C. Lortie, *Schoolteacher: A Sociological Study* (Chicago: University of Chicago Press, 1975).

3 National Center for Education Statistics, "Schools and Staffing Survey (SASS)," 2013 https://nces.ed.gov/surveys/sass/.

4 Mignon Duffy, *Making Care Count: A Century of Gender, Race, and Paid Care Work* (New Brunswick, NJ: Rutgers University Press, 2011).

5 R. C. Bogdan and S. K. Biklen, *Qualitative Research for Education: An Introduction to Theories and Methods*, 4th ed. (Boston: Allyn & Bacon, 2003).

6 Kristin G. Esterberg, *Qualitative Methods in Social Research* (Boston: McGraw-Hill, 2002).

7 Bogden and Biklen, *Qualitative Research for Education*.

8 Sharan B. Merriam, *Qualitative Research: A Guide to Design and Implementation*, 3rd ed. (San Francisco: John Wiley & Sons, 2009), 49.

9 Esterberg, *Qualitative Methods in Social Research*.

10 Brad Olsen and Lauren Anderson, "Courses of Action: A Qualitative Investigation into Urban Teacher Retention and Career Development," *Urban Education* 42, no. 1 (2007), 9.

Bibliography

Alaimo, Katharine, Christine M. Olsen, and Edward A. Frongillo. "Food Insufficiency and American School-Aged Children's Cognitive, Academic, and Psychosocial Development." *Pediatrics* 108, no.1 (2001): 44–53.

American Psychological Association Zero Tolerance Task Force. "Are Zero Tolerance Policies Effective in the Schools? An Evidentiary Review and Recommendations." *American Psychologist* 63, no. 9 (December 2008): 852–862. https://doi.org/10 .1037/0003-066X.63.9.852.

American School Counselor Association. "State School Counseling Mandates and Legislation." 2017. https://www.schoolcounselor.org/About-School-Counseling /State-Requirements-Programs/State-School-Counseling-Mandates-Legislation.

Anagnostopoulos, Dorothea. "The New Accountability, Student Failure, and Teachers' Work in Urban High Schools." *Educational Policy* 17, no. 3 (July 2003): 291–316.

Anderson, Ashlee. "Teach For America and Symbolic Violence: A Bourdieuian Analysis of Education's Next Quick-Fix." *Urban Review* 45, no. 5 (December 1, 2013): 684–700. https://doi.org/10.1007/s11256-013-0241-x.

———. "Teach For America and the Dangers of Deficit Thinking." *Critical Education* 4, no. 11 (October 15, 2013). https://doi.org/10.14288/ce.v4i11.183936.

Andrews, Dorinda J. Carter, Tashal Brown, Eliana Castro, and Effat Id-Deen. "The Impossibility of Being 'Perfect and White': Black Girls' Racialized and Gendered Schooling Experiences." *American Educational Research Journal* 56, no. 6 (December 2019): 2531–2572.

Anyon, Jean. "Social Class and the Hidden Curriculum of Work." *Journal of Education* 162, no. 1 (1980): 67–92.

Apple, Michael W. "Education, Markets, and an Audit Culture." *Critical Quarterly* 47, no. 1–2 (July 2005): 11–29. https://doi.org/10.1111/j.0011-1562.2005.00611.x.

Aronson, Brittany, and Judson Laughter. "The Theory and Practice of Culturally Relevant Education: A Synthesis of Research Across Content Areas." *Review of Educational Research* 86, no. 1 (March 1, 2016): 163–206. https://doi.org/10.3102 /0034654315582066.

Bartlett, Lora. "Expanding Teacher Work Roles: A Resource for Retention or a Recipe for Overwork?" *Journal of Education Policy* 19, no. 5 (September 2004): 565–582.

Basch, Charles E. "Breakfast and the Achievement Gap Among Urban Minority Youth." *School Health* 81, no. 10 (2011): 635–640.

———. "Vision and the Achievement Gap Among Urban Minority Youth." *School Health* 81, no. 10 (2011): 599–605.

Biklen, S. K. *School Work: Gender and the Cultural Construction of Teaching.* New York: Teachers College Press, 1995.

Bloom, Joshua, and Waldo E. Martin. *Black Against Empire: The History and Politics of the Black Panther Party.* Berkeley: University of California Press, 2016.

Bogdan, R. C., and S. K. Biklen. *Qualitative Research for Education: An Introduction to Theories and Methods.* 4th ed. Boston: Allyn and Bacon, 2003.

Cammarota, Julio. "The Gendered and Racialized Pathways of Latina and Latino Youth: Different Struggles, Different Resistances in the Urban Context." *Anthropology and Education Quarterly* 35, no. 1 (2004): 53–74.

Cann, Colette N. "What School Movies and TFA Teach Us About Who Should Teach Urban Youth: Dominant Narratives as Public Pedagogy." *Urban Education* 50, no. 3 (April 1, 2015): 288–315. https://doi.org/10.1177/0042085913507458.

Carnoy, M., and H. M. Levin. *Schooling and Work in the Democratic State.* Stanford, CA: Stanford University Press, 1985.

Carter, Prudence L., and Kevin G. Welner, eds. *Closing the Opportunity Gap: What America Must Do to Give Every Child an Even Chance.* Oxford: Oxford University Press, 2013.

Center for Responsive Schools. "About Responsive Classroom: The Four Key Domains of Responsive Classroom." 2021. https://www.responsiveclassroom.org/about/.

Christie, Christine A., C. Michael Nelson, and Kristine Jolivette. "School Characteristics Related to the Use of Suspension." *Education and Treatment of Children* 27, no. 4 (2004): 509–526.

Cohn, Marilyn M., and Robert B. Kottkamp. *Teachers: The Missing Voice in Education.* Albany: State University of New York Press, 1993.

Collier, Peter J., and David L. Morgan. "'Is That Paper Really Due Today?' Differences in First-Generation and Traditional College Students' Understandings of Faculty Expectations." *Higher Education* 55, no. 4 (April 1, 2008): 425–446.

Collins, Patricia Hill. *Black Feminist Thought: Knowledge, Consciousness, and the Politics of Empowerment.* New York: Routledge, 2000.

Cremata, Edward, Devora Davis, Kathleen Dickey, Kristina Lawyer, Yohannes Negassi, Margaret E. Raymond, and James L. Wentworth. "National Charter School Study." CREDO. 2013. https://credo.stanford.edu/sites/g/files/sbiybj6481/f/ncss_2013_final_draft.pdf.

Darensbourg, Alicia, Erica Perez, and Jamilia J. Blake. "Overrepresentation of African American Males in Exclusionary Discipline: The Role of School-Based Mental Health Professionals in Dismantling the School to Prison Pipeline." *Journal of African American Males in Education* 1, no. 3 (2010): 196–211.

Denavas-Walt, Carmen, Bernadette D. Proctor, and Jessica C. Smith. "Income, Poverty, and Health Insurance Coverage in the United States: 2009," *United States Census Bureau* (September 1, 2010): 60–238. https://www.census.gov/library/publications/2010/demo/p60-238.html

Denham, Susanne A., Kimberly A. Blair, Elizabeth DeMulder, Jennifer Levitas, Katherine Sawyer, Sharon Auerbach-Major, and Patrick Queenan. "Preschool Emotional Competence: Pathway to Social Competence?" *Child Development* 74, no. 1 (February 1, 2003): 238–256. https://doi.org/10.1111/1467-8624.00533.gov.

Department of Agriculture Food and Nutrition Service. "Child Nutrition Programs: Income Eligibility Guidelines." *Federal Register* 77, no. 5 (March 23, 2012). https://www.govinfo.gov/app/details/FR-2012-03-23/2012-7036.

Diamond, Timothy. *Making Gray Gold: Narratives of Nursing Home Care.* Chicago: University of Chicago Press, 1995.

Duffy, Mignon. *Making Care Count: A Century of Gender, Race, and Paid Care Work.* New Brunswick, NJ: Rutgers University Press, 2011.

Eisenberg, Nancy, R. A. Fabes, I. K. Guthrie, and M. Reiser. "Dispositional Emotionality and Regulation: Their Role in Predicting Quality of Social Functioning." *Journal of Personality and Social Psychology* 78, no. 1 (2000): 136–157. https://doi.org/10.1037/0022-3514.78.1.136.

Epple, Dennis, Richard Romano, and Ron Zimmer, "Charter Schools: Research on Their Characteristics and Effectiveness." Working Paper 21256, National Bureau of Economic Research, 2015. https://www.nber.org/system/files/working_papers/w21256/w21256.pdf.

Esterberg, Kristin G. *Qualitative Methods in Social Research.* Boston: McGraw-Hill, 2002.

Food Research and Action Center. "Community Eligibility." 2021. https://frac.org/community-eligibility.

Frisvold, David E. "Nutrition and Cognitive Achievement: An Evaluation of the School Breakfast Program." *Journal of Public Economics* 124: 91–104.

Gardner, Howard. *Frames of Mind: The Theory of Multiple Intelligences.* New York: Basic Books, 2011.

Gay, Geneva. *Culturally Responsive Teaching: Theory, Research, and Practice.* 2nd ed. New York: Teachers College Press, 2010.

———. "Preparing for Culturally Responsive Teaching." *Journal of Teacher Education* 53, no. 2 (March 1, 2002): 106–116. https://doi.org/10.1177/0022487102053002003.

Goleman, Daniel. *Emotional Intelligence: Why It Can Matter More Than IQ.* 10th Anniversary ed. New York: Random House, 2012.

Gordon, Hava Rachel. "'We Can't Let Them Fail for One More Day': School Reform Urgency and the Politics of Reformer-Community Alliances." *Race Ethnicity and Education* 19, no. 1 (January 2, 2016): 1–22. https://doi.org/10.1080/13613324.2014.885430.

Greenblatt, Deborah. "The Consequences of edTPA." *Educational Leadership* 73, no. 8 (May 2016): 51–54.

Guarino, Cassandra M., Lucrecia Santibañez, and Glenn A. Daley, "Teacher Recruitment and Retention: A Review of the Recent Empirical Literature." *Review of Educational Research* 76, no. 2 (June 1, 2006): 173–208. https://doi.org/10.3102/00346543076002173.

Gutiérrez, Lorraine Margot, and Edith Anne Lewis. *Empowering Women of Color.* New York: Columbia University Press, 1999.

Hecht, Amelie A., Keshia M. Pollack Porter, and Lindsay Turner. "Impact of The Community Eligibility Provision of the Healthy, Hunger-Free Kids Act on Student Nutrition, Behavior, and Academic Outcomes: 2011–2019." *AJPH* (August 12, 2020). https://ajph.aphapublications.org/doi/10.2105/AJPH.2020.305743.

Heers, Marieke, Chris Van Klaveren, Wim Groot, and Henriette Maasen van den Brink. "Community Schools: What We Know and What We Need to Know." *Review of Educational Research* (December 1, 2016). https://doi.org/10.3102/0034654315627365.

Heilig, Julian Vasquez and Su Jin Jez. "Teach For America: A Return to the Evidence." National Education Policy Center, University of Colorado Boulder, January 2014. https://nepc.colorado.edu/sites/default/files/tfa-return_0.pdf.

———. "Teach For America: A Review of the Evidence." National Education Policy Center, Boulder, CO, 2010. http://nepc.colorado.edu/publication/teach-for-america.

Hopkins, Belinda. *Just Schools: A Whole School Approach to Restorative Justice*. London: Jessica Kingsley, 2003.

Hossein, Caroline Shenaz. "The Politics of Resistance: Informal Banks in the Caribbean." *Review of Black Political Economy* 41, no. 1 (January 1, 2014): 85–100. https://doi.org/10.1007/s12114-013-9171-9.

Hughes, Michelle, and Whitney Tucker. "Poverty as an Adverse Childhood Experience." *NCMJ* 79, no. 2 (2018): 124–126.

Humphrey, Daniel C., and Marjorie E. Wechsler. "Insights into Alternative Certification: Initial Findings from a National Study." *Teachers College Record* 109, no. 3 (2007): 483–530.

Jackson, Stephanie L., William F. Vann, Jonathan B. Kotch, Bhavna T. Pahel, and Jessica Y. Lee. "Impact of Poor Oral Health on Children's School Attendance and Performance." *American Journal of Public Health* 101, no. 10 (October 1, 2011): 1900–1906. https://doi.org/10.2105/AJPH.2010.200915.

Karp, Melinda Mechur, and Rachel Hare Bork. "'They Never Told Me What to Expect, so I Didn't Know What to Do': Defining and Clarifying the Role of a Community College Student." CCRC Working Paper No. 47, Community College Research Center, Columbia University, New York, July 2012. http://eric.ed.gov/?id=ED535078.

Kleinman, R. E., S. Hall, H. Green, D. Korzec-Ramirez, K. Patton, M. E. Pagano, and J. M. Murphy. "Diet, Breakfast, and Academic Performance in Children." *Annals of Nutrition & Metabolism* 46, no. 1 (2002): 24–30.

Ladson-Billings, Gloria. "Toward a Theory of Culturally Relevant Pedagogy." *American Education Research Journal* 32, no. 3 (September 1, 1995): 465–491.

Lareau, Annette. *Unequal Childhoods: Class, Race, and Family Life*. Berkeley: University of California Press, 2003.

Levine, Susan. *School Lunch Politics: The Surprising History of America's Favorite Welfare Program*. Princeton, NJ: Princeton University Press, 2010. https://press.princeton.edu/books/paperback/9780691146195/school-lunch-politics.

Lortie, Dan C. *Schoolteacher: A Sociological Study*. Chicago: University of Chicago Press, 1975.

Lustick, Hilary. "'Restorative Justice' or Restoring Order? Restorative School Discipline Practices in Urban Public Schools." *Urban Education* (November 14, 2017). https://doi.org/10.1177/0042085917741725.

Maier, Anna, Julia Daniel, Jeannie Oakes, and Livia Lam. "Community Schools as an Effective School Improvement Strategy: A Review of the Evidence." Learning Policy Institute, Palo Alto, CA, 2017. https://files.eric.ed.gov/fulltext/ED606765.pdf.

Massey, Douglas S. *Categorically Unequal: The American Stratification System*. New York: Russell Sage Foundation, 2007.

Mayer, John D., and Casey D. Cobb. "Educational Policy on Emotional Intelligence: Does It Make Sense?" *Educational Psychology Review* 12, no. 2 (January 1, 2000): 163–183.

Mayer, John D., Richard D. Roberts, and Sigal G. Barsade, "Human Abilities: Emotional Intelligence." *Annual Review of Psychology* 59, no. 1 (2008): 507–536. https://doi.org/10.1146/annurev.psych.59.103006.093646.

McNichol, Elizabeth, Douglas Hall, David Cooper, and Vincent Palacios. *Pulling Apart: A State-by-State Analysis of Income Trends.* Washington, DC: Economic Policy Institute, 2012. https://www.epi.org/publication/studies_pullingapart/.

Merriam, Sharan B. *Qualitative Research: A Guide to Design and Implementation.* 3rd ed. San Francisco: John Wiley & Sons, 2009).

Meyers, Alan F., Amy E. Sampson, Michael Weitzman, Beatrice L. Rogers, and Herb Kayne. "School Breakfast Program and School Performance." *American Journal of Diseases of Children* 143, no. 10 (1989): 1234–1239.

Morrison, Brenda, Peta Blood, and Margaret Thorsborne. "Practicing Restorative Justice in School Communities: Addressing the Challenge of Culture Change." *Public Organization Review* 5, no. 4 (December 14, 2005): 335–357. https://doi.org/10.1007/s11115-005-5095-6.

National Alliance for Public Charter Schools. "Unionized Charter Schools: Data from 2018–2019." Washington, DC, December 18, 2020. https://www.publiccharters.org/our-work/publications/unionized-charter-schools-data-2018-2019.

National Center for Education Statistics. "Characteristics of Public School Teachers." *Condition of Education*, U.S. Department of Education, Institute of Education Sciences, 2020. https://nces.ed.gov/programs/coe/indicator_clr.asp.

———. "Characteristics of Public School Teachers Who Completed Alternative Route to Certification Programs." *Condition of Education*, U.S. Department of Education, Institute of Education Sciences, 2018. https://nces.ed.gov/programs/coe/indicator_tlc.asp.

———. "Public Charter School Enrollment." *Condition of Education*, U.S. Department of Education, Institute of Education Sciences, 2020. https://nces.ed.gov/programs/coe/indicator_cgb.asp.

———. "Racial/Ethnic Enrollment in Public Schools." *Condition of Education*, U.S. Department of Education, Institute of Education Sciences, 2020. https://nces.ed.gov/programs/coe/indicator_cge.asp.

———. "School Nurses in U.S. Public Schools." U.S. Department of Education, Institute of Education Sciences, April 30, 2020. https://nces.ed.gov/pubsearch/pubsinfo.asp?pubid=2020086.

———. "Schools and Staffing Survey (SASS)." 2013. https://nces.ed.gov/surveys/sass/.

No Kid Hungry. "Hunger in Our Schools." 2015. https://www.hungerinourschools.org.

Oliver, Kimberly L., and Rosary Lalik. "The Body as Curriculum: Learning with Adolescent Girls." *Journal of Curriculum Studies* 33, no. 3 (May 1, 2001): 303–333. https://doi.org/10.1080/00220270010006046.

Olsen, Brad, and Lauren Anderson. "Courses of Action: A Qualitative Investigation into Urban Teacher Retention and Career Development." *Urban Education* 42, no. 1 (2007): 5–29.

Osterman, Karen F. "Students' Need for Belonging in the School Community." *Review of Educational Research* 70, no. 3 (September 1, 2000): 323–367. https://doi.org/10.3102/00346543070003323.

Power, Michael. "Making Things Auditable." *Accounting, Organizations and Society* 21, no. 2–3 (February 1, 1996): 289–315. https://doi.org/10.1016/0361-3682(95)00004-6.

Preston, J. A. "Domestic Ideology, School Reformers, and Female Teachers: School-teaching Becomes Women's Work in Nineteenth-Century New England." *New England Quarterly* 66, no. 4 (1993): 531–551.

Richardson, Jason, Bruce Mitchell, and Juan Franco. "Shifting Neighborhoods: Gentrification and Cultural Displacement in American Cities," *National Community Reinvestment Coalition* (2019). https://ncrc.org/gentrification/.

Rothberg, Iris C., and Joshua L. Glazer, eds. *Choosing Charters: Better Schools or More Segregation*. New York: Teachers College Press, 2018.

Rury, J. L. "Who Became Teachers? The Social Characteristics of Teachers in American History." In *American Teachers: Histories of a Profession at Work*, edited by D. R. Warren, 9–48. New York: Macmillan, 1989.

Salovey, Peter, and Daisy Grewal. "The Science of Emotional Intelligence." *Current Directions in Psychological Science* 14, no. 6 (December 1, 2005): 281–285.

Salovey, Peter, and John D. Mayer. "Emotional Intelligence." *Imagination, Cognition and Personality* 9, no. 3 (March 1, 1990): 185–211. https://doi.org/10.2190/DUGG-P24E-52WK-6CDG.

Saltman, Kenneth J. *Capitalizing on Disaster: Taking and Breaking Public Schools*. Cultural Politics & the Promise of Democracy. Boulder, CO: Paradigm, 2007.

Sanchez, Claudio. "Obama's Impact on America's Schools." NPR, 2017. https://www.npr.org/sections/ed/2017/01/13/500421608/obamas-impact-on-americas-schools.

Sanderson, Donna R. "Transiency, Test Scores, and the Public: One School District's Story." *Studies in Educational Evaluation* 30, no. 3 (2004): 225–236.

Schiele, Jerome H., M. Sebrena Jackson, and Colita Nichols Fairfax. "Maggie Lena Walker and African American Community Development." *Affilia* 20, no. 1 (February 1, 2005): 21–38. https://doi.org/10.1177/0886109904272012.

Scholastic and Bill and Melinda Gates Foundation. "Primary Sources: America's Teachers on Teaching in an Era of Change." 3rd ed. Scholastic and Bill & Melinda Gates Foundation, 2013. https://eric.ed.gov/?id=ED562664.

Shore, Cris. "Audit Culture and Illiberal Governance: Universities and the Politics of Accountability." *Anthropological Theory* 8, no. 3 (September 1, 2008): 278–298. https://doi.org/10.1177/1463499608093815.

Skiba, Russell J., Mariella I. Arredondo, and Natasha T. Williams. "More Than a Metaphor: The Contribution of Exclusionary Discipline to a School-to-Prison Pipeline." *Equity & Excellence in Education* 47, no. 4 (2014): 546–564. https://doi.org/10.1080/10665684.2014.958965.

Smith, Dorothy E. *Institutional Ethnography: A Sociology for People*. The Gender Lens Series. Walnut Creek, CA: AltaMira, 2005.

Southern Education Foundation. "A New Majority: Low Income Students Now a Majority in the Nation's Public Schools. Research Bulletin." 2015. https://files.eric.ed.gov/fulltext/ED555829.pdf.

Swidler, Ann. "Culture in Action: Symbols and Strategies." *American Sociological Review* 51, no. 2 (April 1, 1986): 273–286. https://doi.org/10.2307/2095521.

Teach For America. "Internships and College Programs." 2021. https://www.teachforamerica.org/how-to-join/internships-and-college-programs.

———. "What We Do." 2021. https://www.teachforamerica.org/what-we-do.

Thomas, M. Shelley, Shantel Crosby, and Judi Vanderhaar. "Trauma-Informed Practices in Schools Across Two Decades: An Interdisciplinary Review of Research." *Review of Research in Education* 43 (March 2019): 422–452.

Tronto, Joan C. *Caring Democracy: Markets, Equality, and Justice*. New York: New York University Press, 2013.

U.S. Department of Education. "Executive Summary of the No Child Left Behind Act of 2001." Legislative Materials; Abstracts, November 20, 2007. http://www2.ed.gov/nclb/overview/intro/execsumm.html.

———. "No Child Left Behind: A Toolkit for Teachers." Pamphlets, August 13, 2009. https://files.eric.ed.gov/fulltext/ED483139.pdf.

———. "Race to the Top Program: Executive Summary." Washington, DC, November 2009. http://www2.ed.gov/programs/racetothetop/executive-summary.pdf.

———. "Title I, Part A Fact Sheet." Pamphlets, March 9, 2006. https://www2.ed.gov/rschstat/eval/disadv/titleI-factsheet.html?exp=0.

U.S. Government Accountability Office. "No Child Left Behind Act: Education Should Clarify Guidance and Address Potential Compliance Issues for Schools in Corrective Action and Restructuring Status." GAO-07-1035, September 5, 2007. https://www.gao.gov/products/GAO-07-1035.

Vincent, Claudia G., Tary J. Tobin, Leanne S. Hawken, and Jennifer L. Frank. "Discipline Referrals and Access to Secondary Level Support in Elementary and Middle Schools: Patterns Across African-American, Hispanic-American, and White Students." *Education and Treatment of Children* 35, no. 3 (2012): 431–458.

Weinreb, Linda, Cheryl Wehler, Jennifer Perloff, Richard Scott, Davis Hosmer, Linda Sagor, and Craig Gunderson. "Hunger: Its Impact on Children's Health and Mental Health." *Pediatrics* 110, no. 4 (2002): 1–9.

Wells, Amy Stuart, Alejandra Lopez, Janelle Scott, and Jennifer Jellison Holme. "Charter Schools as Postmodern Paradox: Rethinking Social Stratification in an Age of Deregulated School Choice." *Harvard Educational Review* 69, no. 2 (December 31, 2009): 172–205. https://doi.org/10.17763/haer.69.2.k34475n478v43022.

Welner, Kevin G., and Prudence L. Carter. "Achievement Gaps Arise from Opportunity Gaps." In *Closing the Opportunity Gap: What America Must Do to Give Every Child an Even Chance*, edited by Prudence L. Carter and Kevin G. Welner, 1–10. Oxford: Oxford University Press, 2013.

Winicki, Joshua, and Kyle Jemison. "Food Insecurity and Hunger in the Kindergarten Classroom: Its Effect on Learning and Growth." *Contemporary Economic Policy* 21, no. 2 (2003): 145–157.

Yosso, Tara J. "Whose Culture has Capital? A Critical Race Theory Discussion of Community Cultural Wealth." *Race, Ethnicity, and Education* 8, no. 1 (2005): 69–91.

Index

About the Author

KATIE KERSTETTER is a research affiliate with the Center for Social Science Research at George Mason University. She collaborates with nonprofit and community-based organizations on research projects to support food access, nutrition education, and maternal and child health. She has a PhD in sociology from George Mason University and a master's in public policy from the University of Maryland College Park.